INDIAN BUREAUCRACY
Maladies and Remedies

INDIAN BUREAUCRACY
Maladies and Remedies

HAR SWARUP SINGH

SHIPRA

ISBN: 978-81-7541-376-4

First Published in India in 2007

Indian Bureaucracy: Maladies and Remedies

Published by:
SHIPRA PUBLICATIONS
115-A, Vikas Marg, Shakarpur
Delhi-110092, INDIA
Phone: 91-11-65277210, 91-11-22500954
Fax: 91-11-22458662
E-mail: info@shiprapublications.com
www.shiprapublications.com

PREFACE

Bureaucracy plays a significant, indeed pivotal, role in economic and social advancement of a nation, especially a developing one. As stated by Kofi Annan, former Secretary General of the United Nations, "Good governance is perhaps the single most important factor in eradicating poverty and promoting development." I could see it in my early government career that civil servants play a key role in the country's progress but the realization was heightened when I went to the United States for further studies (at North Carolina State University at Raleigh). The courses I took, especially in economic development, welfare economics, and the history of economic thought (wherein the history of developmental concepts — capitalism, socialism/ communism and mixed-economy systems — and the attendant governance and control mechanisms were studied and debated) improved considerably my understanding of the role of bureaucracy. My analytical faculties were strengthened by the rigorous course work and interactions with an outstanding group of teachers — in particular with my major professor, Dr. Lee R. Martin, who had been a student of Prof. John Kenneth Galbraith at Harvard and had worked in Pakistan for about a year as part of a Harvard University economic advisory team. During our discussions of obstacles to economic growth, Prof. Martin often lamented the rigid administrative structure with which the Indian sub-continent had been saddled as a hangover from the days of imperial rule.

After finishing my formal studies, I kept up with the study of developmental issues in my various assignments where — as I moved up the career ladder — administration started to claim more attention, and over time to overtake my concentration on economic research. I gained some administrative experience in my job as an international civil servant for over two decades but more of it was to come later— in ample measure and with copious doses of complexity — when I returned to work in India during the mid-1980s through mid-1990s. My first job at a leading state university — CCS-Haryana Agricultural University at Hisar — and three subsequent senior political appointments — made me think deeply about the governance structure and procedures, and about doing something by way of improving efficiency and democratic functioning in the domain of my responsibilities. On a personal note, I am grateful to the nation for providing me an opportunity to serve in privileged positions — an experience I will always cherish.

I wish to emphasize that I have thought for a *very long time* about what would constitute an effective and responsive governance structure and about what could be done to develop the country — at a faster pace — for which we do not lack the potential in human or material resources. Many of the quotations and extracts I have used in this study come from the original material — paper cuttings, journal & magazine articles, official reports, and books — that I have been carefully saving for several decades. To illustrate, I have on file a series on "ICS and I" that appeared in *The Illustrated Weekly of India* well over forty years ago! The papers have yellowed and are somewhat frayed but it has been a pleasure to re-read those articles by numerous outstanding members of the ICS; for one thing, it seems they all could write well.

Besides the study of the subject of bureaucracy and bureaucratic reforms and my direct experience as an administrator, official/personal interactions with some outstanding civil servants (belonging to the ICS and the IAS &Allied Services) — who have been elders/mentors, co-workers, and friends — have also helped me understand the problems that our civil service encounters and the opportunities it provides. These individuals included Dharma Vira, Khub Chand, Dr. M.S. Randhawa, S. Tarlok Singh, M.G. Kaul, and T.N. Kaul (all belonging to the ICS), and Bhagwan Singh (one of the earliest members of the IAS). All of these illustrious civil servants, who were proud of their Service, felt strongly that the bureaucratic system needed to be changed — to adapt to the requirements of development. A large number of other bureaucrats at different levels (from Cabinet Secretary down to district-level bureaucrats) have also contributed to my understanding of the fundamentals and processes of governance; I have referred to the views of a number of them at appropriate places.

Moreover, I have learned a good deal from many public men, especially some *thinking* politicians with whom I had the privilege of working. I have also appreciated the views of some others with whom I did not have an official relationship; quotations have also been included from the insightful writings of some of them — Mani Shankar Aiyar and Arun Shourie, just to name two.

While I was actively thinking about putting together my ideas on bureaucratic reforms, along came an invitation to present a Paper at a seminar on "The Role of Bureaucracies in Economic Development and Foreign Affairs." The event was organized jointly by Deen Dayal Upadhyaya Foundation, the U.S.–India Forum, and the School of Public Policy at George Mason University (GMU), Fairfax, Virginia. Incidentally, GMU — known for its impressive work on economic policy and public administration — currently has not one but two Nobel Prize winners in its Economics Department! I am including the press release issued at the conclusion of the seminar on bureaucracy as an appendix at the end of the book.

My presentation at that gathering actually formed the nucleus of this book. The post-seminar discussions and further thinking about, and study of, unfolding developments in the country's governance encouraged me to expand the narration of ideas contained in the original seminar Paper.

A number of my knowledgeable friends have been kind enough to read the book manuscript — at evolving and/or final stages and offer valuable suggestions. They include Dr. Walter Andersen, Acting Director of the Asia Program at Johns Hopkins University's School of Advanced International Studies (SAIS), and a former political counselor at the U.S. embassy in New Delhi and senior India/South Asia expert in the U.S. State Department; Gautam Bambawalé, IFS, Minister, Political at the Indian Embassy in Washington, D.C.; Anil Gupta, IPS, Minister, Personnel and Community Affairs at the Embassy; and Ajai Singh Sirohi, a well-regarded consultant in strategic management, who had earlier worked with three leading U.S. corporations — IBM, Allied Signal, and Honeywell International. After going through the manuscript, these distinguished diplomats/experts found time to discuss — more than once — the various key issues I had dealt with and provided friendly encouragement. To them, I express heart-felt thanks for time and ideas so generously given. I am indebted to three other individuals who were also supportive and gave helpful comments on the book draft: Dr. Betsy Singh, a noted research scientist and a former professor/dean of medical research, now heading the Boss Research Consultant Group in Virginia; Surendra Pal Singh, a civic-minded, investigative journalist based in Ghaziabad, U.P.; and Dr. Krishna Banaudha of George Washington University (GWU), Washington, D.C., a young teacher and researcher in the important field of molecular biochemistry, who had earlier been associated with India's Central Drug Research Institute at Lucknow.

However, while I have benefited from insightful comments received from the above-named individuals and from earlier interactions with many other knowledgeable people, I accept full responsibility for the analysis, judgments arrived at, and recommendations made in the study.

I do realize that the subject of bureaucracy and its reforms is vast in scope. To deal with it comprehensively is not only daunting but impossible for an individual because of the limitations of time and one's capacity to analyse the myriad factors single-handedly, and then come up with meaningful suggestions for improvements. Despite these constraints, I am venturing to present my views and share my modest expertise in administration, based on my interest in the subject and its study for a long time, and the experience I gained at senior levels — in international civil service and diplomacy; in economic planning at national and local levels (policy formulation, program/project development, and also in guiding their execution); and in direct, hands-on management as the chief executive of a leading university and a Union Territory.

Baisakhi, April 13, 2007 **Har Swarup Singh**

CONTENTS

I

INTRODUCTION

Government, even in its best state, is but a necessary evil; in its worst state, an intolerable one.

— *Thomas Paine*

Bureaucracy[1] has a very long history in India but other societies, too, created bureaucracies out of necessity. In Egypt's *Old Kingdom* (some 5,000 years ago), for instance, bureaucracy was a key factor in the inception of its renowned civilization.[2] Bureaucrats were expected to have tact and good manners, and display humility. It is perhaps for this reason that Egyptian officials were called *civil servants,* a designation that governments have adopted down through the ages. China has had a large bureaucracy for a long time with officials selected on the basis of merit; thus, in the Seventh Century A.D. government job applicants had to write essays about Confucian philosophy and compose poetry! This practice gave chance even to a lowly peasant to become a mandarin.[3]

In the *Vedas* and epics (*Ramayana and Mahabharata*), there are many references to the duties of various office-holders and overall responsibilities of a just ruler. Kautalya describes the traits of a good ruler in *Arthashastra*: "In the happiness of his subjects lies his happiness, in their welfare, his welfare; whatever pleases himself, he shall not consider as good but whatever pleases his subjects he shall consider as good." Information is also available on the administrative set-up in the Maurya and Gupta dynasties; Ashoka the Great was assisted by a well-structured bureaucracy (not just the army establishment, which he used ferociously before turning into a pacifist and renouncing violence altogether). Much later, the Mughal emperors built upon the existing systems. Akbar, another great ruler in India's history, had a superb administrative machinery and a legendary Council of Nine Advisers (*Navratna* or nine jewels). In fact, the land settlement and revenue system developed by Raja Todar Mal, Akbar's revenue minister, was so good that its main features were adopted by the British and these remained basically unchanged until India's Independence in 1947.

The British East India Company, of course, made changes in the system of governance to suit its needs. After the government in London took direct charge of India, it set up the Indian Civil Service (ICS) — the steel frame of the imperial rule. For many years, members of the ICS (considered *heaven-born*) used to be Englishmen but, with nationalistic feelings burgeoning in the country, the government started taking Indians into the ICS — though grudgingly and slowly. However, from 1923 onwards — when competitive examinations for the Service were allowed to be held in India (rather than in London alone) — the proportion of Indian officers in the ICS increased steadily.[4]

After Independence, Congress Party leaders (especially Pandit Jawahar Lal Nehru and Sardar Vallabh Bhai Patel) decided to keep the basic ICS structure and gave it key governance responsibilities.[5] In his book on Sardar Patel, B. Krishna describes the vision that Patel had for the civil service. His concept emerged from the belief he held and which he once expressed to his Home Secretary, H.V.R. Iyengar: "It would be a bad day if people did not look up to officials holding high positions. Ministers come and ministers go, but the permanent machinery (the civil service) must be good and firm, and have respect of the people." Nearly a hundred years earlier, Lord Macaulay had expressed in the British Parliament similar views with regard to the ICS, referring to the importance of character of a civil servant. Patel looked upon the successors of the ICS as 'partners with him in the task of administration.'[6]

The inherited administrative machinery performed admirably — under very difficult circumstances — handling serious responsibilities related to partition of the country (division of assets and liabilities and in controlling violence); refugee resettlement; integrating the princely states into India; setting up planning and scientific research institutions; and initiating economic & social development. The last group of activities relating to development was never given priority by the British who had concentrated on control, law and order issues, and exploitation of India's resources for their own benefit.

The ICS had, in fact, set an excellent tradition over the years. In the words of G.D. Khosla, an eminent member of the Service: "The real substance of this tradition consisted of a high standard of integrity, a whole-hearted devotion to duty, and a mental and physical discipline which enabled the members to concentrate on their administrative duties."[7] Incidentally, according to D.W. Brogan, the ICS was regarded 'uniquely honest and competent' not only in India but in the whole of Asia.[8]

The government of free India started new civil services — Indian Administrative Service (IAS) and Allied Services — and their members adopted the better traditions of the ICS. They acquitted themselves well for decades, working diligently, honestly, and with dedication influenced, in part, by the conduct of political leaders of the time — freedom fighters who had sacrificed much and had suffered no end in their passionate quest for Independence.

However, slowly, efficiency in governance began to slide. The results of non-performance by our civil services during recent decades are now glaringly obvious. Although bureaucrats alone are not responsible for India's overall economic and social backwardness, they certainly share a significant part of the responsibility. Data on economic and social well-being in India indicate that:

- Over one-fourth of India's population is still trapped in degrading poverty. While the county's GDP is rising at a fast rate — averaging 8 per cent in the past three years[9] — its benefits are not shared widely; the pronounced disequilibria in growth sectors/locations are reflected in a widening gap between the rich and poor segments of the population, and between rural and urban areas.[10]
- Health indicators remain in a low range and some 70 per cent of the population lacks adequate sanitation facilities. A large number — estimated at 170 million — does not have access to potable water. Healthcare is woefully inadequate, especially in rural areas where a mere 21 per cent of the population has access to primary healthcare. India is home to more than one-third of the world's malnourished children and approximately 2.5 million children die annually. As a result of poor nutrition and limited healthcare facilities, life expectancy — at 64 years — is still unacceptably low.
- Only slightly more than 70 per cent of the male population is literate (compared to 98.9 per cent in China, for instance) and female literacy remains around 50 per cent. Moreover, many *literates* cannot do much more than sign their names.

The country's infrastructure for development — except perhaps in the IT sector — is inadequate to handle the projected growth. Apart from roads connecting some major cities — Delhi, Agra, Jaipur, etc. — the road network is unsatisfactory. India's seaports and airports, with one or two exceptions, have antiquated facilities. Forget world standards, parts of our transportation infrastructure look very much like the facilities in some of the least developed countries. The energy situation — rising costs and insufficient supplies — is undoubtedly a matter of great concern. Thus, massive investments are needed to improve the country's infrastructure. During a recent two-day conference in New York (headlined by a former U.S. Ambassador to India, Robert D. Blackwill, and India's Minister of State for Industry, Ashwini Kumar), it was stated that "sustaining and taking forward economic growth in India demands, by one estimate, an investment of $1.5 trillion. In the infrastructure sector alone more than $240 billion is projected."[11] For the power sector an infusion of $140 billion is required during 2002–2012 to meet the target of 40,000 MW of power generation. Infrastructure indeed plays a pivotal role in attracting foreign direct investment (FDI) and unless serious attention is immediately paid to solving current problems, our hopes of becoming a developed nation will remain chimerical.

That India has to do a much better job than in the past in attracting FDI can be seen with reference to the country's performance *vis-à-vis* that of tiny Singapore. As of 2005, India had received $45 billion in foreign direct investment, with $8 billion of that from the United States. Singapore, by contrast, received more than $186 billion, of which $48 billion came from the U.S.![12]

It may be added that high rates of economic growth — current and projected (even higher) — make many people forget the overall economic reality; the *relative* rate of growth in income claims attention and not the equally relevant *absolute* level of income. Thus, a recent issue of *Foreign Affairs* refers to India as "a roaring capitalist success story." The Economic Times matches the accolades calling recent growth "a harbinger of economic superstardom." Such "India Shining" hype sidesteps the fact that the country's $728 per capita GDP is just slightly higher than that of sub-Saharan Africa. And, even poor Haiti— by far the most impoverished country in the western hemisphere and a nearly failed state — has a per capita income of $1740! Furthermore, the *U.N. Human Development Report* for 2005 indicates that, even if high current rates of growth in India are sustained, it will not catch up with high-income countries within this century.

Obviously, a lot remains to be done and, while celebrating recent achievements, one should not get carried away by complacency-generating myths of economic superstardom. As a high priority, the base of economic activity has to be widened and diversified. A significant part of the growth that is currently taking place in the information technology, business processing, and a few other sectors, has largely been *jobless.* To find employment for the fast-rising younger population, India will have to pay increased attention to stimulating growth in the labour-intensive manufacturing sector that, historically, has powered economic advances around the world.

In addition to the functional shortcomings of bureaucracy, a marked deterioration has also set in ethical standards in India (greater among politicians than in civil services), with corruption creeping even into the highest echelons of bureaucracy. To quote Khosla again: "To the Indian Civil Service and the traditions built up by its members over the years, I owe whatever virtues I acquired as a public servant. And it distresses me to think that the tradition is dying with the Service. If the volume of complaints against public servants is any indication of reality, the present day official would seem to belong to a wholly different species of civil servants."[13] Many factors account for the current unsatisfactory state of affairs: the mismanagement and misbehaviour on the part of political masters; rigid rules & regulations and undue control of economic activities; lack of accountability for civil servants; increasing materialism; and decline in the general standard of morality in civil services and in society at large.

That Indian bureaucracy now is in *urgent* need of reforms is widely recognized by our political leaders, businessmen, professionals, civil servants themselves, and especially the ordinary members of the public who suffer because of indifferent, inefficient, and dishonest civil services. The situation is as bad as, if not worse than, even in some of the least developed and highly corrupt countries of the world. The suffering public in India is by now used to refusal of entitled services and arrogant behaviour of public servants, and many no longer feel the sting of rejections and insults. However, it is painfully noticed, or felt directly, by foreigners and visiting/returning Indians. A recent story in a New York weekly describes the experience of a young Indian-American who came to work as a short-term volunteer with an NGO in Mumbai and was distressed to learn that her disabled and handicapped students faced hurdles every day — "Hurdles that I had never before imagined." She had unpleasant meetings with officials from the Mumbai Municipal Corporation while trying to effect some needed changes in city slums. This made it clear to her why her parents "always use the word 'ineffective' to describe the Indian government machinery."[14]

Apparently, what was said earlier of the all-British Indian Civil Service (ICS) — that they were neither Indian nor civil, and certainly not servants of the public — still applies in a very high proportion of cases (except that bureaucrats now are Indian, but many still regarding themselves as *Brown Sahibs*). To paraphrase Shakespeare: Something is rotten in the state of India.[15]

The everyday unhappy experiences of people in all walks of life have made some respected leaders and experts react with disappointment and resentment, and to pronounce some harsh truths. Take, for instance, the experience of none other than His Excellency Dr. A.P.J. Abdul Kalam, President of India, when as a scientist he was heading the Satellite Launch Vehicle (SLV)-III project and was frustrated due to procurement delays caused by the indifference and red-tape tactics of the Controller of Accounts. To quote from his autobiography:

> "I was determined to fight the inertia built into the [bureaucratic] system before I found myself being dragged down with it. I asked myself a practical question: Could one live with these insensitive bureaucrats? The answer was a big No."[16]

Over the years, such feelings have been echoed — in varying degrees — in other societies as well.[17]

No wonder, civil services in India are not being rated well in terms of attitude and originality in thinking. According to S.N. Chary, a study — which surveyed the perception regarding IAS officers across several sections of co-workers, such as police officers, technocrats, academics, and professionals — came out with negative findings: "The IAS officers got the lowest rating on being visionary and the next lowest rating on innovation and creativity." Interestingly, they got the top rating on 'projecting self as an expert on most things.' Some other notable 'high' ratings received by them were for being 'power-hungry, manipulative, arrogant, and inaccessible.'[18] Basing on personal experience of attitudinal surveys, one would not rule out a degree of bias in the above results — introduced by professional rivalries, by respondent selection. Nevertheless, it cannot be denied that there is a serious image problem for civil services. One of the top civil servants — B.K. Chaturvedi, the Cabinet Secretary — acknowledges that such a problem does exist for Indian officials: "The bureaucracy's image has been diminished because it is generally felt that bureaucrats are not upright and fair."[19] Dedicated members of civil services are truly concerned about their image problem, and more than that, about the underlying rot. As M.G. Devasahayam, a former IAS officer — pained by the decline in standards in civil services — puts it: "It is unfair and uncharitable to allow such a splendid instrument (All-India Services) to decline, decay and degenerate inch by inch and render itself irrelevant. It may even be prudent to consider winding up of the Service than to allow it to languish and its conscientious incumbents squirm in anguish everyday."[20] S.N. Chary, too, was inclined towards the disbandment of all-India services: "The IAS and other civil services as they exist today need a total revamping or even a phased disbandment."[21]

However, one can settle for a substantive, meaningful revamping of civil services and *not* disbandment; there is no need to get carried away and throw the baby out with the bathwater. In terms of quality — intelligence and capability — India has a good civil service cadre and so the country needs to basically worry about how to restructure and improve the *system.* This, in many areas, would involve taking drastic measures to achieve the level and quality of performance for which the potential definitely exists.

It is not that the governments in the past had not worried about the unsatisfactory state of affairs — for they had, appointing many commissions/committees for administrative reforms, and working groups aplenty! But nothing or very little ever happened by way of improvements. The reports have been gathering dust (and attracting termites), which reminds the author of an observation by a British ICS officer that was repeated by a senior Indian civil servant friend while discussing the appointment of yet another committee or commission. Though slightly tasteless, the aptness of the comment impels one to quote:

"Commissions are like commodes;
first there is a sitting,
then there is a report, some noise,
and then the matter drops!"

In any case, various commissions and task forces have produced a lot of information on bureaucracy. A large volume of additional material is contained in other reports, books, monographs, academic papers, and popular articles. And, yes, a plethora of information is now available on the Internet: *Google* search yielded nearly 1.3 million items on *Bureaucracy!* Looking for *Bureaucracy in India,* turned up about 157,000 items; narrowing the search further to *Bureaucratic Reforms in India,* ended up with some 41,200 entries. With so much material available, one can manage to study only a limited number of items, and at best, look at the remaining material selectively.

The insight into governance processes both at macro and micro levels, particularly in different posts that the author had the privilege of holding in India, was valuable indeed. Naturally, in high-level appointive positions one has to deal with the political leadership, which makes the person appreciate the need for interactive and collaborative relationship between the political bosses in a democracy and the bureaucrats whose role is to execute the policies laid down by the former. At the same time, it is well accepted, and is indeed desirable, for senior-level bureaucrats to tender their considered and frank advice at the policy formulation stage. It is a different matter that many politicians do not accept such advice and, more often than not, want the advice to be tailored to agree with their views and to meet their own narrow and selfish agendas. Dharma Vira, a distinguished member of the ICS (who had served as Cabinet Secretary, ambassador, and governor) talks about the problem in his autobiography — *Memoirs of a Civil Servant* — citing his experience of working with V.K. Krishna Menon who tried to make his life miserable on account of what Menon termed *lack of cooperation* on the part of Dharma Vira. Actually, the latter had *worse* stories to narrate in personal conversations; some more views of Dharma Vira are cited later.

The author benefited a good deal from his personal, non-official association with some older civil servants belonging to the ICS and with numerous senior members of the IAS and Allied services.[22] Working with some dedicated political leaders was a learning experience, too, besides being — in a few cases — inspirational. One, of course, always learns from co-workers, consciously or otherwise. And, as indicated earlier, when the manuscript was ready, the author had the good fortune of getting valuable comments from some friends with regard to coverage and the message he was trying to convey.[23]

But all said and done, the author owns full responsibility for the analysis presented in this book and for all prescriptive suggestions.

It may be added that the analysis of, and remarks about, the country's bureaucracy basically relate to All-India Services — IAS, IFS, and Allied Services — as these are the pre-eminent civil services. Because of the time constraint it has not been possible to look at bureaucracy as a whole, which is a huge entity. Besides the central services, such as the Secretariat Service, it comprises State civil services (Provincial Civil Service, PCS, in Uttar Pradesh, Rajasthan Administrative Service, RAS, and so on); State technical services, e.g. Provincial Medical Service (PMS) in Uttar Pradesh; district/sub-divisional employees; and block and village-level workers. They all are bureaucrats, but the administrative structure, duties and responsibilities, challenges and opportunities, and working conditions and rewards vary in scope and quality from level to level.

Further, the coverage of topics in the book is selective, with emphasis placed on subjects that appear to be of paramount importance in the context of reforming India's bureaucracy.

II

IN DEFENSE OF BUREAUCRACY[1]

Bureaucracy is an inevitable complement to democracy.
— *Joseph A. Schumpeter*

Before proceeding with comments regarding the shortcomings of India's civil service and suggested reforms, it may be stated that the problems are *systemic* and minimally *personal.* As observed by Mani Shankar Aiyar: "the cause is not to be found in individuals."[2] The country has kept a number of features of the civil service of the colonial era — its structure and many operational procedures — and have also made some undesirable modifications to the old system. Politicians have felt free to mishandle and manipulate the administrative machinery. Still, members of the All-India services — IAS, IPS and others — generally continued to display, for a few decades after Independence, a sense of commitment to the nation's progress. Our civil servants are, by and large, intelligent and well informed and have tried to retain many sound values, especially devotion to the rule of law. This is happening despite the onslaught from above — from political masters, many of whom do not seem to be bothered about adhering to rules and regulations. Once, when K.L. Punjabi, ICS, Secretary of the Ministry of Agriculture at the Centre, explained to his minister that if the latter departed from procedures, he would open floodgates of group and individual pressures, the minister said petulantly: "What is [the] use of my being a Minister if I can not oblige some of my friends?"[3]

It seems the ministers are extremely happy when officials stoop to concur! Madhav Godbole, IAS, a former Union Home Secretary, has made some pertinent observations with regard to the behaviour of politicians: "The Information and Broadcasting Minister K.P. Singh Deo had reportedly laid down certain ground rules for the functioning of civil servants in his ministry — 'Servants should not speak till the master permits' and 'you are not to apply your mind, you are just to do what you are told' ...T.N. Seshan colourfully described civil servants as 'call-girls' and 'backboneless wonders' ...The master-servant syndrome was always there in the psyche of political masters who often believed they personified the State...There is a total lack of understanding or appreciation of the role of civil servants... Everything is being done to undermine, weaken and thus hasten the demise of civil services." Godbole concluded that without the undercutting of civil services' role and responsibilities "one would have not seen such sharp decline in institutional standards, practices and ethos governing the civil services."[4]

In sharp contrast to the likes of K.P. Singh Deo and V.K. Krishna Menon, stood out the approach of Sardar Vallabh Bhai Patel who had clearly stated: "My Secretary can write a note opposed to my views. I have told them: If you do not give your honest opinion for the fear that it will displease your minister, then, please you had better go. I will bring another secretary. I will never be displeased over a frank expression of opinion." That civil servants in those days could disagree with, and oppose, the views of the minister can be illustrated by no better example than Home Secretary H.V.R Iyengar noting his opposition on the file for the creation of Andhra Pradesh as a linguistic state. The proposal had been advanced on the basis of a resolution on the subject by the Congress Working Committee comprising Pandit Jawahar Lal Nehru, Dr. Rajendra Prasad, Maulana Abul Kalam Azad, and Sardar Patel himself! Patel had told Iyengar: "It must make no difference to you who are the parties to the Congress Working Committee Resolution. You must clearly and frankly analyse the whole problem." Iyengar did exactly that subjecting the proposal to 'cold analysis.' As a result, the proposal was postponed; in fact, such a linguistic state could never materialize as long as Patel was alive.[5]

Besides pressures from above — ministers and others — there have been temptations from below (from businessmen and others, many of whom seek undue favours day in and day out) to weaken and corrupt the bureaucracy.

Still, democracy would not have taken root and prospered in Independent India without the conscientious efforts of our civil servants who — for many years — obstinately strove to do the right thing in conformity with the laws, prescribed procedures, and healthy traditions. There has been, on some occasions, *political instability* in the country but administration has been characterized by relative *stability* and *cohesion* because we had in place a functioning, albeit imperfect, bureaucratic machinery. One need not belabour the point: Just look at other developing countries — in the neighbourhood and elsewhere. How many working democracies can you spot in Asia, Africa, Latin America, and Eastern Europe? In the realm of upholding democratic values, India has indeed been a shining beacon! A substantial proportion of the electorate has regularly and freely exercised voting rights, and the counting of votes — manually and in electronic voting machines — has been free of noticeable flaws. Yes, there have been cases of 'booth capturing' and election-related violence but, generally speaking, we still compare favourably even with some developed countries in terms of democratic functioning. Nani Palkhivala — in his *Vision of India* — rates democracy a great achievement in a country "where nearly a billion people, more than the combined population of Africa and South America, live together as one political entity under conditions of freedom. Never before in history, and nowhere else in the world today, has one-sixth of the human race existed as a single free nation. Professor Rostow of Texas University regards the survival of Indian democracy as the most important phenomenon of the post-war era."[6] In the concluding part of his *Vision,* Palkhivala is confident about the long-term future of the country.[7]

In the present era of political instability — of coalition government after coalition government — a good civil service is very much needed to provide stability in the nation's governance and to foster fast economic growth. This underscores the importance and urgency of bureaucratic reforms. That India's civil services recruit from a pool of bright aspirants is the general opinion. In the words of Arun Shourie, ex-minister and a reputed journalist, "We still have individuals who are outstanding by every standard. But the system chisels every creative impulse out of them."[8]

Members of All-India Services with whom the author dealt in various capacities — collaborative and consultative — were, on the whole, a very good group to work with. In fact, a number of them, especially those who worked with him in Pondicherry Union Territory (U.T.), went beyond the call of duty in discharging their responsibilities.[9] Several highly desirable goals were achieved because of sustained efforts on the part of the U.T.'s bureaucracy (from Chief Secretary Subhash Sharma down to the lowest level) to translate the plans and aspirations into concrete action.[10]

Thinking of the role of bureaucracy, one may recall what had happened at the national level a decade-and-a-half ago. Dr. Manmohan Singh and P. Chidambaram, important ministers, utilized the bureaucracy effectively in the process of launching the now widely lauded economic reforms. The venture would not have succeeded had they shown a lack of will and persistence, and importantly, had there not been competent executors of the policy — civil servants like N.K. Singh. However, generally speaking, for things to happen in the present administrative system in India, a lot more than guidance is needed — exhortation, prodding, sustained monitoring, and so on — because *the system lacks a developmental orientation and is not self-generating in terms of creative ideas.* For civil servants there is no internal trigger for trying new ideas and for more-than-routine activity. There are no, or only small, rewards for initiative and bold action; and there also is no punishment for non-performance and irresponsible behaviour. The concept of accountability is, by and large, absent in the country's civil service; this subject is discussed in some detail later.

So far as political leaders are concerned, most show little interest in development and welfare activities, and extend little support to bureaucracy in these areas; their interests lie elsewhere, especially in winning the next election, and any vision for a bright future they tout is forgotten soon after coming to power. In a large number of cases, changing political bosses seem to have an *unchanging* agenda — personal enrichment and self-perpetuation. Too bad they have to misuse bureaucracy for this ulterior purpose!

To reiterate what was said at the beginning of this section: comments about the shortcomings of civil services — and a good many will be pointed out — should be seen in the *systemic* schema. Efforts should be made to reform the system. Madhav Godbole makes a pertinent observation in this context in another article: "There is undeniably a great deal that is wrong with the Indian bureaucracy, or *Babudom* as some would prefer to call it (with a supercilious connotation). But it has to be realized that it too represents all that is wrong with every other section of society. The marriage of the bureaucracy with society has to work. Deriding the partner day in and day out will only complicate matters, leading to further erosion of trust."[11] So, there is need to undertake meaningful, far-reaching reforms of the system; the country needs a governance machinery that is better — substantially better — than what is there at present, and the sooner this is accomplished the better it would be for the nation.

III

LACK OF SPECIALIZATION IN CIVIL SERVICES

No man undertakes a trade he has not learned, even the meanest, yet every one thinks himself sufficiently qualified for the hardest of all trades — that of government

—*Socrates*

India's colonial-era model of delivering government services has been unable to serve public needs in a democracy. As stated in a Loksatta Discussion Paper: "There is gross administrative incompetence, corruption, insensitivity and unresponsiveness, completely alienating the people from governance…Functioning of the bureaucracy is the most disturbing feature of our polity as far as the people are concerned. This has left an ever-increasing gulf between expectation and reality and the enormous erosion of legitimacy of the political process."[1]

The present administrative structure has proved to be noticeably deficient to meet the needs of the future, especially in the field of development. The change in the system of governance is needed because of changed circumstances: fast industrial growth taking the economy towards post-industrial era; emergence of technology as a driver of growth; revolution in information technology and the overall knowledge sector; and increasing globalization marked by significant inter-country movement of capital, labour, and other resources. The nation has to move boldly into the Twenty-first Century global economy aiming to strengthen Indian society and enable the masses to live up to their full potential in a vibrant democratic setup.

Coming to the specific ills of Indian bureaucracy, a substantial handicap has been the *lack of specialization.* This persisting feature (generalist civil services) is a key legacy of the Indian Civil Service of the Raj days, but not the only one. As will be discussed in later chapters, the country has retained several other obsolescent and undesirable features, including administration/control-centric approach; insularity and elitism, characterized by pomp and show and the enabling power and perks; and lack of transparency and accountability. Unfortunately, the similarities with the ICS are more in structure and form and not in substance: While those 'heaven-born' administrators were uniquely reputed in the domain of their specified duties (not generally geared for development of the country) for *efficiency* and *integrity,* far too many of the new breed of civil servants are known for *inefficiency* and *corruption.*

The *new guardians* — the members of the Indian Administrative and Allied Services — are usually all-purpose *generalists* rather than *specialists.* A member of the IAS, like the earlier ICS officer, may be posted as director of civil aviation one time; his next appointment could well be in urban housing or forestry (he/she may not be able, in some cases, to differentiate even between commonly found trees); then the officer may get the department of arts & culture or agriculture (the officer may not know that groundnut/peanut is an underground crop).[2] The IAS members are found everywhere — in specialized jobs where professional qualifications are highly desirable or a *sine qua non.* They are occupying a large number of these and other senior posts, which they got encadred (reserved) for themselves. Thus, they run steel plants, electricity boards, port trusts, development authorities, All-India Radio, *Doordarshan* (television), and so on. They also get a large share of foreign assignments; many times, they stay there for good.

Members of the IAS and Allied Services also manage to get appointed as heads of institutions of higher learning even when they lack academic credentials or aptitude. This author has personally known a number of IAS and Allied Services officers who worked as university vice chancellors (presidents) and did not seem — for obvious reasons — to fit in the academic environment.

Brig. N.B. Grant mentions in this connection that "till recently, the post of Comptroller and Auditor General, which used to be held in the past by officers of the Indian Audit and Accounts Service, was held by an IAS officer. It is on record that in U.P. an IAS officer also officiated as the District Medical Officer, in the absence of the latter on leave![3] Similarly, Angana Parekh points out that for 2½ years the Director General (DG) of the venerable Archeological Survey of India (ASI) was an IAS officer who did not possess the required technical qualifications. "The recruitment rules made it impossible for senior, well qualified ASI officials to be eligible for the DG's post."[4]

In addition to laying claims to regular jobs, the bureaucrats (members of the IAS and other All-India Services) even manage to get a lion's share of slots in commissions and committees appointed by the government. According to Joginder Singh, a distinguished police officer who knows the ways of the government well having worked as head of intelligence: "Whenever a committee, commission, or [another] body is set up, how it is that only retired government employees are appointed to it? Whether it is a Banking Recruitment Commission…or any Grievances Board, or Tribunal, it is filled only with the retired or retiring Government employees. Whenever any new body is created, the first objective of the official pushing through its case, is to make sure that a job is there to fill up when he retires."[5]

Such dominance/monopoly of jobs was in order for members of the ICS when *administration* and *control* were key responsibilities and not *development* and *welfare.* But times have changed. With substantial advances in every field, especially in science and technology, knowledge of the subject matter on the part of civil servants has become extremely important — actually a *must* in a substantial number of jobs. Though not so crucial, such knowledge would be helpful even to the policy-making politician.

Dharma Vira had not been happy for years with the prevailing state of civil services: "The tasks of the services now are much more complicated and diverse. We are now pledged to establish a welfare state…The service structure has, however, continued to remain practically unchanged. One would have thought that with changes in the types of work, ideology and objectives of the services, modifications in the method of recruitment, training and procedures in the services and the administration would be introduced. But this has not happened and the changes made are just marginal and do not go to the root of the problem."[6]

The value of specialized training should really not be debatable in modern times. To illustrate, the author found that as vice-chancellor of a State Agricultural University knowledge of agriculture was extremely helpful. It was gained through early college studies in agriculture and farm management before shifting to economics/ agricultural economics and sociology; also, farming background was a significant contributor to the understanding of agrarian/rural issues. Because of the need for such specialization, vice-chancellors of agricultural universities have *usually* been agricultural scientists or specialists in related sciences; individuals even with the highest academic/intellectual achievements and fame in the field of humanities are *not* appointed as heads of such institutions. The only exceptions seem to have been several clout-wielding IAS officers, and frankly, such appointees were generally regarded as usurpers and seldom embraced by the faculty. In many situations in an agricultural university it is *imperative* to be knowledgeable at least about broad areas of research and extension (the two areas that, along with education, form the mandated core of responsibilities of an agricultural university — on the pattern developed for the U.S. Land Grant State Universities). One important example is the setting of priorities for research and extension programs. Of course, there are some administrative responsibilities where knowledge of agriculture may not be strictly required — e.g. office management and enforcement of personnel rules, etc; in any case, such duties are handled by administrative & accounts officers, comptroller, and the registrar under the vice-chancellor's overall guidance. For these jobs, a civil servant (member of the IAS or PCS) would do all right[7], but *not* for the position of vice-chancellor. An institution of higher learning should rightly be headed by someone with suitable academic/scientific credentials.[8]

Of course, there are *exceptional* people (including civil servants) who would do well in a wide range of leadership roles — at a university or elsewhere. Two future presidents of their nations come to mind for having served as respected university presidents — K.R. Narayanan at Jawahar Lal Nehru University in Delhi[9] and General Dwight D. Eisenhower at Columbia University in New York. Their outstanding abilities and stature brought recognition to the universities (attracting grants and other funding, and acting as a magnet for renowned faculty) and served as a counterbalance to the relative lack of academic credentials. However, *usually* even non-technical universities/institutions (with arts/science specializations) should be headed by academic people — accomplished educationists, other men of letters, and scientists — *not* by regular bureaucrats.

In most countries, civil services are highly specialized entities. Thus in the United States, civil servants in the Department of Agriculture (USDA) are specialists in agriculture (and related sciences), agricultural economics, statistics/econometrics, and ancillary fields (with lawyers, personnel managers, P.R. specialists, etc. for sections needing their expertise).[10] Similarly, the U.S. Commerce Department has its own civil service; the delegate(s) from that department to the international organization with which the author was associated at the time were trade/legal experts with considerable experience in international trade, commodity agreements, enforcement of contracts, and the like. Transfers from one cabinet department (ministry) to another are unusual.

In India, we have moved very slowly and reluctantly towards establishing specialized Services. For instance, the Indian Economic Service (IES) was started years ago but its members have complained of discrimination in assignments and outside deputations. Now, agricultural scientists are being selected by the Agricultural Scientists Recruitment Board (ASRB) to fill jobs in the institutes and agricultural research centres run by the Indian Council of Agricultural Research (ICAR). The post of Secretary of the Department of Agricultural Research and Education (DARE) is held, ex-officio, by the Director General of the ICAR. However, the secretary of the main agriculture department usually is an IAS officer rather than an agricultural scientist-administrator.[11] It may be added that there is a fair-sized pool of candidates — in the ICAR system, elsewhere in agriculture departments, and in agricultural universities — from which credible selections of the Secretary to the Central Ministry of Agriculture could, and ought to, be made.

Prime Minister Indira Gandhi had, years ago, appointed technically qualified people as secretaries of some departments. Subsequently, also, technical people have been holding such jobs but a substantial number of prestigious, top posts still go to IAS officers (as these have been reserved for them — encadred) and not to technocrats.

A severe dearth of promotional opportunities beyond middle- and some upper middle-levels has had a demoralizing effect on technical people who saw the IAS members and other generalist bureaucrats abrogating to themselves the right to occupy top positions where financial rewards, perks & powers, and recognition were far more attractive than those available to technocrats. To illustrate, an agricultural scientist who joins the agriculture department in a state, or at the Centre, could aspire eventually — towards the end of service career — to become Director of Agriculture/Commissioner. Of course, very few would ever go to that level. An IAS officer, in sharp contrast, would occupy that or a similar position after 10-15 years of service. And, members of the IAS and Allied Services do not have to wait for a job opening for their promotions, which are time-bound. Moreover, technical people usually are not appointed secretaries of departments in the State or at the Centre. This used to be the case in Haryana, U.P., and a number of other states and — quite likely — continues to this day.

The same situation prevails in the case of doctors and engineers. Also, in many states (perhaps most), the performance report (annual confidential report, ACR) for senior technical people in the district used to be written by the IAS collector who may be half as old as the district engineer or doctor and may also be drawing much lower emoluments[12]; this happens because members of the IAS have to finish the district assignment (as collector/deputy commissioner) within a decade of service or less. It is thus obvious that technocrats are neither recognized nor rewarded for their service, lagging considerably behind regular bureaucrats — on any relevant criterion. *This state of affairs clearly shows how the nation belittles the contribution made by technical people.* Severe limitations on the opportunities available to technically qualified individuals rob us of their potential contributions to nation building; the prevailing situation also creates a lot of heart burning and demoralization, thereby affecting employee productivity.[13] Most technocrats routinely, and unhappily, retire from relatively less privileged and less rewarding jobs.

So what happened in this highly iniquitous situation? The new generation of graduates of engineering, medicine, agriculture, and other technical subjects reluctantly decided to desert their fields of specialization and started appearing for civil service examinations. There was a confluence of *push factors* (lack of promotional opportunities and recognition, and lower salaries in technical careers) and *pull factors* (highly attractive service conditions — security, prestige, and financial rewards — in the IAS and Allied Services) working to make technical people opt for All-India civil services in preference to their chosen fields of study. One engineer, while he was abandoning his specialized field and taking the civil service examination, reportedly justified his decision in these terms: "As an engineer I will only be building bridges and not having much recognition and rewards for my work, but as an IAS officer I may be requested — say, as a Divisional Commissioner — to inaugurate one of those bridges as the *chief guest!*"

Charulata Joshi, in an article in *New India Digest,* quotes a senior official in the Central Electricity Authority, New Delhi (who preferred anonymity): "The domination of IAS is a symptom of our colonial hangover. If vital policy decisions relating to specialist fields are going to be taken by generalists, it is better that these (technical) professionals lay their degrees aside and join the ranks of bureaucracy." In fact, such sentiments have been expressed for many years and the number of technical people entering civil services has been rising significantly. Upmanyu Chatterjee, a civil servant (and a very good writer — in one book, *English August: An Indian Story,* he talks about the Indian Administrative Service) then with the Ministry of Human Resources Development, finds the brain drain from technical fields disturbing; Joshi quotes him: "The government spends a lot of money subsidizing education in the IITs and in the medical and engineering colleges. If, after acquiring a degree, these professionals join the civil services, it is a tremendous waste of government money." The same article by Joshi cites other specific views and experiences which account for the exodus of technocrats to civil services. K.V. Radhakrishna, a medical graduate, joined the Indian Revenue Service in 1987 as that appeared to be 'the fastest route to financial security'; Prem Nath Tiwari, who worked for some years as an electronics engineer, grabbed the chance to enter civil service when the age limit for competitive examinations was raised and he succeeded in getting into the customs service in 1991. He made the change because of the feeling that he was stagnating in his previous job: "There was no satisfaction in doing routine, maintenance work. And there was all-pervading fear that I would never reach the top rung of my organization. That post is generally reserved for a bureaucrat." Prof. S.R. Maheshwari of the Indian Institute of Public Administration said that such technical entrants into the civil service know that "all vital decisions pertaining to their careers will be taken by IAS men." More power, status ('aura'), and a huge dowry ('Today the civil servants command the highest figure'[14]) were the other factors specifically advanced as attractions of the civil service.[15]

Another journalist — Monica Uppal — who also talked to a number of successful candidates with engineering degrees, reported similar attractions of the civil service. Thus, K.J. Singh was influenced by 'the glamour of status and the authority to take big decisions.' The desire to be part of the policy-making setup persuaded Arshinder Chawla while a rewarding vista of job opportunities and an urge for social recognition drove Ram Chopra to opt for the bureaucracy. Another engineer commented: "No one beyond his factory premises recognizes an engineer, whereas an IAS officer gets a salute wherever he goes." The social system obviously attaches a higher status to a civil servant than to an engineer or a doctor. According to Satinder Pal Kaur, who stood by her husband during his grueling preparation for the civil service examination, "a civil service pay may be less but the perks and public recognition are better than…in a private firm."[16]

Most candidates thus gave truthful responses to why they had left their specialized fields after years of hard study and considerable government expenditure on their training. But one also heard phony answers like 'joined civil service to serve society/humanity' (a response rendered meaningless due to frequent use). Wouldn't utilizing their engineering or medical training for designing and building dams, bridges, office complexes, and machines, or attending to human suffering by removing pain and healing patients constitute service to people? Aren't science/technology *nerds* and computer *geeks* making momentous life-altering advances for society's betterment?

Granted that civil service salaries do not always compare well with those in the private sector, particularly during recent years of increasing globalization, but this is not deterring a number of aspirants who, in fact, do not look at the salary as much as they look at other factors including the chance of earning on the side a lot of money, in corrupt ways. In this context Sonali Verma quotes K.B. Lall, ICS: "A government servant can never be paid enough these days…It's the availability of easy money that draws them to the civil service." Verma, too, refers to the huge dowry an IAS officer commands, adding that it is just the tip of the money iceberg; "Bureaucrats are reputed to be showered with money and gifts," for doling out favours.[17]

Losing a significant number of technically qualified people to generalist bureaucracy, at a seemingly accelerated pace, amounts to a huge waste of taxpayer funds as the highly subsidized, education of a doctor or an engineer involves big financial outlays and takes a very long time. Unfortunately, the engineer/doctor-turned-bureaucrat will most likely be doing the work where his technical knowledge is neither required nor utilized. B.K. Chaturvedi, the Cabinet Secretary, acknowledges the serious problem of non-utilization of technical expertise in civil services: "The government feels that a sizable amount of money is spent to train doctors and engineers. It is a waste to acquire such specialized skills and then come to the civil services where these skills are not required. Thus it is important to ensure that there is proper allocation of resources, both at a human and financial level."[18] Incidentally, the minimum educational qualification for IAS and Allied Services is only an undergraduate degree — B.A., B.Sc., etc.[19]

Perhaps the most debilitating feature of technically qualified people becoming bureaucrats is the loss of creative potential in technical fields — in research and application of scientific and technological advances that would have been possible had the better students stayed in their chosen technical fields. In Haryana Agricultural University when there was a clamour for officially helping agricultural science students to prepare for civil service examinations — through financial help for coaching, arranging lectures by experts (internal and external), and holding mock interviews, etc. — the author reacted unfavourably: Why do agricultural scientists after years of hard, technical study at considerable government expense want to become generalist civil servants? Why should an agricultural university (and a reputed one) harm its own interests, and those of agricultural sciences at large, by facilitating the movement of its promising students — the *crème de la crème* — to vocations where their specialized training would be wasted? Hadn't Haryana Agricultural University made — along with Punjab Agricultural University and a few others — substantial contributions to India's Green Revolution? Wouldn't letting go of their brightest amount to devaluing the specialized instruction being imparted at considerable cost?[20] However, in several meetings, some professors, advisers, and a very large number of students persuaded the author to give in because of the *much brighter future* the university's students would have as bureaucrats *vis-à-vis* their careers as agricultural scientists, extension specialists, and educationists.[21]

In the mid-1990s, some Tamil Nadu universities introduced a 'foundation course' in degree programmes to help students do well in the All-India civil service examinations because, according to the then education minister: "The performance of students from Tamil Nadu in IAS and IPS examinations is dismal." Such a course was tried out, for example, at Manonmanian Sundaranar University.[22] These moves appear ill advised. Universities and other places of higher learning should concentrate on *learning* and not become coaching centres for civil service examinations. Emphasis on competitive examinations is likely to dilute the existing course work and would certainly be a drag on advanced degree programmes and research. Are all students interested in taking civil service examinations?

Wouldn't there be a demand also for coaching courses for banking officers and excise inspectors? The universities and colleges had better leave coaching to Brilliant Tutorials, S.N. Dasgupta (Coaching) College, and other coaching centres/shops and concentrate on doing a better job of meeting their own mandates. In that job most institutions are falling sadly short of providing quality education and are happily churning out unemployable graduates in ever-increasing numbers. The only exceptions to this unsatisfactory performance are the reputed technical/specialized institutions: the IITs, IIMs, State Agricultural Universities, and a large number of medical colleges admitting students on a competitive basis; the IIT, in particular, has now become a quality brand in the West, especially in the United States.

That the best, technically qualified students are leaving their specialized fields would be clear by looking at the top performers in civil service competitions, which, to begin with, are highly competitive. Thus in 1993, there was a clean sweep by engineers for top positions — 18 out of the top 20 qualifiers for the IAS were engineers, and one was a doctor. The number of doctors seems to have gone up since then. In 1996, of the 638 successful candidates, *professionally qualified* persons (engineers, doctors, agricultural scientists, etc.) accounted for as much as 40 per cent; 45 per cent came from the humanities stream; and the remaining 15 per cent from sciences. Of the overall total, more than half belonged to the reserved quota categories.[23]

However, as stated earlier, the expertise of the professionally qualified people is not being put to use in the civil service setup. The lack of need for high-level technical expertise in the IAS and Allied Services, the structure and functioning of civil services, and policies for allocation of personnel[24] are factors that come in the way of utilizing technical/specialized knowledge; alas, such expertise is going to inexcusable waste!

To correct this situation (losing valuable technical people to generalist services), suggestions have been made to bar engineers, doctors, agricultural scientists, and other technically qualified individuals from entering IAS and Allied Services. But this would be a wrong step, reminding one of H.L. Mencken's saying to the effect that most complex problems have solutions that are simple, easy, and wrong! The country really has to tackle the root cause: *the great attraction of civil services relative to the much less satisfactory career opportunities available to technical people.*

The security and prestige associated with government posts and lack of appreciation for the private sector on the part of earlier generations were typified by the unfavourable reaction of the author's father at the time of his job change in 1961 — from a nice research job in the prestigious National Council of Applied Economic Research to an economic advisory position with a big unit of Sir Shri Ram Group — Delhi Cloth & General Mills Company — at an appreciably higher salary in the relatively new and challenging field of business economics.[25]

To retain technical people in their own fields the country will have to provide them comparable service conditions (salaries, perks, power, and social respect) in their own fields as available to generalist civil servants; then the problem would be solved automatically. Technical people, of course, deserve this fair treatment, and more importantly, the country needs their specialized services to accelerate economic progress. They have proved their competence and potential by doing as well as, or better than, non-technical people in civil service competitive examinations. Incidentally, their outstanding performance took the wind out of the sails of the wrong notion held by arts & science graduates entering the IAS and Allied Services during the early post-Independence period that they were, somehow, academically superior to technically qualified people who were not usually appearing for civil service competitions at the time.

The point being made is important enough to bear repetition: Please extend recognition and rewards to technocrats and let all, or a substantial majority of them, work in their own technical/specialized fields in the interest of India's development. Don't force them to join generalist services where their expensive training has little use. There is no valid argument that would justify the present unfair and lopsided system that heavily favours generalist bureaucrats and treats technocrats in a step-motherly fashion — not only in material terms but also in terms of social recognition and appreciation of their contributions.[26]

IV

ESTABLISH ADDITIONAL TECHNICAL/ SPECIALIZED SERVICES

> *Government functions are increasingly complex...[and] demand domain expertise, specialization, sector experience, and deep insights. The colonial practice of recruiting an all-purpose generalist service is both archaic and dysfunctional.*
>
> —Jayaprakash Narain, *Loksatta*[1]

The handicap of a *generalist* bureaucracy can be taken care of by setting up more All-India Services of *specialized* nature and treating them *on a par* with the IAS and Allied Services. Actually, there were a number of technical/specialized Services even during the administration/control-oriented Raj days. In early decades of the past century, there were nine All-India Services — the Indian Civil Service, Indian Police Service, Indian Educational Service, Indian Medical Service, Indian Service of Engineers, Indian Agricultural Service, Indian Veterinary Service, Indian Forest Service, and Indian Forest (Engineers) Service. The changes that subsequently took place in the All-India Services are described below, drawing heavily on an excellent historical narrative by T.K.A. Nair (a senior civil servant) in a guest article that appeared in a leading Daily.[2]

The Government of India Act, 1935, provided for the continuance of the ICS, IPS, and Indian Medical Service under the era of provincial autonomy, stipulating that appointments to these Services shall continue to be made by the Secretary of State for India. The decision to create All-India Services for Independent India was taken in the Conference of Provincial Premiers in October 1946 on the eve of Independence. Against the background of the pro-active developmental role assumed by the government after 1947, the Ashok Chandra Report (1954) recommended the constitution of new All-

India Services in technical fields; however, this has not been achieved in any significant way to this day.

The States Reorganization Commission (1953-55) had also looked into the role and relevance of All-India Services in the context of its recommendations regarding the creation of linguistic states. It also felt that *"executing developmental projects necessitated that technical personnel be recruited and trained ... having uniform standards of efficiency and the feeling of belonging to common and important cadres."* The Commission, therefore, recommended the creation (revival) of the Indian Forest Service, the Indian Service of Engineers, and the Indian Medical and Health Service. A Conference of State Chief Ministers held in August 1961 approved this list of new services, observing that "the formation of all-India services would strengthen national integration." The Rajya Sabha passed a resolution for the creation of these three additional services; this was followed by the passage of an Act by Parliament in December 1963. During discussions on the legislation it was highlighted that these Services "would help develop an all-India outlook." As a follow-up, the Indian Forest Service was constituted in July 1966 with the participation of all States. However, despite protracted efforts, the other two Services of the old (The Indian Service of Engineers — Irrigation, Power, Buildings and Roads — and the Indian Medical and Health Service were not created because of non-cooperation on the part of certain State governments. Later on, the Administrative Reforms Commission fully endorsed the concept of All-India Services.

The Estimates Committee of the Seventh Lok Sabha, too, examined the concept and the functioning of All-India Services and presented a detailed report in April 1984. The Committee expressed unhappiness at the fact that "although it was decided to create All-India Services in Engineering and in Medicine/Health as far back as 1963, these services could not be constituted due to hesitation on the part of some States." The Committee expressed the hope that those States would soon see the usefulness of these Services; if that did not happen, the Committee requested the government to examine "whether these Services could be constituted covering the States which have already signified their consent, leaving the remaining States to join the scheme later."

The Commission on Centre-State Relations (1983-88), popularly known as the Sarkaria Commission, also examined at length various aspects of All-India Services and confirmed that there was "vital need for these Services." It referred to "the tremendous increase in development activities of government and the growing emphasis on the welfare aspects [that] have placed the government administration both at the Union and State levels under severe strain," and added that "the performance by the public services in general has, from the point of view of the public, fallen much short of expectations."

There are now six important specialized Services that had existed in the Raj days but have not been reconstituted:

— Two that had been recommended more than forty years ago: The Indian Medical Service (Civil) and the Indian Service of Engineers (Irrigation, Power, Buildings and Roads), and
— Four others that were not considered worthy of revival by Independent India but that, nonetheless, espouse development and welfare: The Indian Education Service; Indian Agricultural Service; Indian Veterinary Service; and the Indian Forest (Engineers) Service.

Of these, the last two could, in fact, be combined with the Indian Agricultural Service and Indian Forest Service, respectively; this would mean that the revival of old, Raj days' Services would be limited to only two — the Indian Educational Service and Indian Agricultural Service — both being extremely important. Education decidedly plays a key role in the transformation and development of any society. And, agriculture in India is a key sector of the economy, providing livelihood to around three-fourths of the population, and still accounting for a significant share of the national income. Setting up of these two Services and two others (Medical and Engineering) that had been recommended over forty years ago is of pivotal importance in the developmental context. While creating these Services the country also has to consider what *additional* Services would be required to meet the needs placed on the governance system by: the growing IT sector; latest scientific and technological advances; galloping globalization; and any other need(s) arising from unforeseen developments having a bearing on administration.

Independent India has, in fact, given in — albeit hesitatingly — to the creation of new Services, additional to the IAS and Allied Services (the latter include the Indian Foreign Service which first takes toppers from the combined competitive examination; IPS; Indian Audit and Accounts Service; and Services to handle Income Tax,

Customs, etc.). Thus, years ago, the Indian Economic Service was established but its role and powers fall short of the status granted to the IAS. When the author joined the Planning Commission as a Member in late 1989, one of the first groups to meet him comprised some members of the Indian Economic Service (including the son of a professor at the university that he had just left). They all complained about the step-motherly treatment meted out to them by the government.[3]

An All-India Forest Service exists but its members, too, are not contented. Although they are serving in the technical field of their choice for which they had received good training, they do not get due recognition and rewards.[4] A number of them keep appearing for the IAS and Allied Services examinations and some get selected. One of them who had left the forestry career after getting into the Customs Service was taken on deputation by the author to work as his P.S. in the Planning Commission. A bright individual, this scientist could have contributed more to the nation's overall welfare by staying in the Forest Service, perhaps by increasing the forest cover, working to check global warming, and protecting our environment — more desirable activities one would think than worrying about customs duties and smuggling. And, he would have stayed with forestry, his first love, had the government's policies not made technical services inferior to the IAS and Allied Services. His action seemed like a case of: *If you can't beat them join them.*

An All-India Agricultural Service can be created easily by utilizing the nucleus of agricultural scientists in the Indian Council of Agricultural Research (ICAR) system, in State Agricultural Universities, and in other specialized institutions. Currently, agricultural scientists for the ICAR-run institutes and research stations, and the senior staff of the ICAR itself are being recruited by the Agricultural Scientists Recruitment Board (ASRB) at New Delhi — sort of Union Public Service Commission (UPSC) for agriculture.[5]

If technical/specialized services are established, their members will work as professionals — engineers, doctors, agricultural scientists/extension workers, and so on — *not* as generalist administrators. All existing technical people working in the government at the all-India level can be easily absorbed in relevant Services (as was done when the Indian Economic Service was created).

To reiterate, the main suggestion here is to create additional technical/specialized Services and to give recognition to their members on a par with members of the IAS. Then we would be able to attract and retain suitable entrants who would be able to devote their energies to developmental work; there would be no pre-eminent service like the IAS to direct them from a higher perch, as is the case now when a substantial number of senior-most positions are the monopoly of the IAS. This would, of course, also take care of inter-service rivalries. In his autobiography, T.N. Kaul talks specifically about this unhealthy practice of the IAS dominating all civil services: "What is…important is to prevent the monopoly of power and important posts that has now been concentrated in the IAS. A few scientists, technologists, and economists have been brought in here and there but they are in a small minority and most important Secretariat posts such as Secretaries (Additional, Joint, Deputy, and Under Secretaries) are held by the new steel frame of the IAS who band together against all outsiders. They lay claim even to ex-cadre posts at the Centre. It has become a vested interest and discriminates against even outstanding entrants from outside the IAS."[6]

The domination by the IAS is not limited to having plum posts alone; their salaries —which start at the same level as those of other All-India Services initially — go up more as they get promoted. The annual increments in the IAS are marginally higher but the real difference is noticed later. The IAS officers when promoted to senior/selection grades are put in a pay-bracket higher than that of other officers of All-India Services. They also achieve promotions earlier and manage to go to more top positions compared with those in other Services. Julius Ribero (a senior member of the IPS), who has analyzed these discriminatory trends, has this to say: "Most, indeed almost all IAS officers, attain the rank of Secretary to the Government of India or Chief Secretary (CS) or Additional Chief Secretary to State Governments after 30 years of service. The vast majority of IPS officers and those of other Central Services retire on a lower grade. Only a handful of them rise to the Secretary level. In fact, Secretary-level jobs were denied to them till the last decade." Ribero's reaction to the demand of the IAS Officers' Association that they should start on a 30-per cent higher pay than officers of other Services was: "[The demand] is obviously intended to establish the [Indian Administrative] Service's superiority over other sister Services. It is this notion of 'superior' and 'inferior' that has caused problems all along. In this day and age such notions will be rejected...Actually, there is no reason to perpetuate the superiority of any one service over another. Each has its role to perform and should be proud of the work it does for the public good."[7]

To be fair, all Services should be treated as *equal*. However, this would not preclude a *coordination* role being assigned to member(s) of a particular Service, as appropriate, when circumstances warrant such action; but this would not make the coordinating individual/ Service *superior* and the others, *inferior.* Pankaj Vohra makes a relevant point in this context: "Qualification of an examination at a particular level during the earlier stages of a person's life does not imply that the person for the rest of his or her serving career is going to exhibit the same sort of brilliance."[8] The argument has been taken further by the author, later on, by saying that current competitive examinations, *per se,* do not measure very well the characteristics desired in civil services. Thus, significant modifications are needed in the examination system. Obviously, the challenge would be to improve the testing system *without, in the least, compromising merit* through introducing any bias or other factor(s) that may tilt the playing field. And, testing should not be uniform for all Services since the traits needed for satisfactory performance vary from Service to Service, sometimes significantly.

All the recommendations made in this section are based on the need for a changed orientation — *highlighting development vis-a vis administration.* Most high-level jobs, of course, have both elements but the emphasis needs to be shifted to development and welfare, making it the key component of a bureaucrat's responsibilities. *The much smaller cadre of the IAS officers (as a corollary to the establishment of technical/specialized Services) should man departments/offices where administration/management is the key component of an officer's duties. (Still, they should know about development and understand its basic issues and concerns.)* This would mean assignment to posts where management, finance, and related matters are the main job requirements. Tata Administrative Services (TAS) apparently follows a system of this type.[9]

Mani Shankar Aiyar (a Central Cabinet Minister, outstanding journalist and writer, and — more importantly in the present context — a former member of the Indian Foreign Service) feels strongly about the need for a significantly shrunken IAS cadre: "The IAS must be slashed into a Secretariat Service. ... And the sweetener we can — indeed must — offer the IAS is vastly increased salaries in exchange for smaller (albeit *Mandalized*) numbers…The best and the brightest of the *Mandalists* would then run our secretariats freed of the necessity of taking bribes."[10]

The much larger cadre of the technical/specialized officers, by contrast, should man departments/offices where development is the key component of an officer's duties. (Still, they should know about administration and understand its basic issues and concerns.)

A part of the training of all Service probationers could remain common — as is the case now. The present pattern of training could be modified and streamlined in keeping with the suggested development-centric orientation. It may be emphasized that administration is easier to teach to the probationers than imparting technical knowledge that took technically qualified candidates (engineers, doctors, agricultural scientists, and others) very many years to acquire.

For entry at senior levels for technocrats (that is recommended later), administrative experience generally should pose no problem as most of them would have handled administration. The type of people suggested for consideration — a university vice-chancellor, a senior executive from industry or business, a chief conservator of forests, a dean or director of research from a university[11], or a senior officer from a government department — must have already devoted a significant amount of time to administration. Still, if is felt that they fall short on some measure of administrative proficiency, special make-up training could easily be arranged. Short-term courses could be designed for technocrats at the Lal Bahadur Shastri Academy at Mussorie, the Administrative Staff College at Hyderabad, or other academies that have lately been set up at various universities and other places.

Having a number of additional Services would relieve the competitive pressure generated by examinations for All-India Services. The intake would be larger and entrance tests would also cover additional subjects. Some papers can be common but others will have to be geared to testing the knowledge of — and aptitude for — technical/specialized subjects, according to the Service that the candidate wishes to join. Group discussions and interviews should be designed/improved (to cover more ground and go a bit deeper) to assess a candidate's suitability, keeping in mind the attributes needed/desired for job performance in a particular Service.

At the moment, some candidates spend *years* in preparing for competitions; unfortunately, moving up the maximum age for entry (to 28, and 35 for reserved categories; the minimum age is 21 years) gives more time to candidates for cramming up information; rote learning seems to benefit candidates under the present examination system. There is a very large number of cases where the candidate prepares for 2, 3 or more years, appearing as many times as allowed and doing nothing else during that period. Not only a vast majority of candidates do not succeed in clearing the hurdles in one go, those who do succeed in getting into Allied Services appear in the examination — again and again — to get into the IFS or IAS. No wonder appearing in the annual civil service examinations is now referred to as the *national pastime* of the young! The amount of time, energy, and resources devoted to this venture in which a substantial number of candidates never succeed (ending up highly frustrated, demoralized, and — many times — financially broke) is clearly a colossal, inexcusable waste.

Raising the age limit for entry and allowing multiple chances helps especially those who have the wherewithal to devote years to get into the civil service, making the system inequitable. Those with resources are able to maintain themselves while also getting the benefit of group coaching, having private tuitions, and buying books, magazines, competition guides, and other material considered helpful. To illustrate the point, the topper in the IAS and Allied Services examinations in 1995 — who came from a family of reasonable means — seems to have devoted two (or more) years to concentrate on preparations, appearing more than once; he did not think he was all that great a student in his M.A. Economics course at Delhi University. Asked if he had topped in that examination, too, his reply was: "Oh no … I just managed 56 per cent." Studying in isolation, he put in about 14 hours a day. "It was the life of a hermit," he recalled and added that had he got the IPS in the previous year, he would not have bothered to take the examination again; he improved his position through concentrated study from 229th rank in the previous year to the top rank.[12] In another interview also he emphasized how hard he had worked: "I was literally confined at home 24 hours including on festivals such as *Diwali*."[13] Apparently, spending more time contributed more to his laudable success the second time than did his cerebral endowment.

Success after competition-oriented study for several years shows that the examination system puts a premium on acquired knowledge and rote learning — cramming the facts — rather than measuring the innate intelligence and ability of a candidate; the latter attributes seem much more important for success in senior civil service jobs than *book smarts.* In the selection of best candidates, it is important to consider *multiple intelligences* and not just success in acquiring knowledge. The idea of multiple intelligences was elaborated upon some two decades ago by Howard Gardner, Professor of Education at Harvard University, who felt that musical, athletic, and other talents are separate from, but as important as, high Scholastic Aptitude Test (SAT) scores (this academic assessment is used in the United States for admission to colleges). Gardner called the academic test as measurement of linguistic intelligence and logico-mathematical; the other intelligences are: spatial, musical, bodily kinesthetic, interpersonal, and naturalist. And it is not guaranteed that people who are smart in one category would be smart in others as well.[14]

Robert Sternberg, a Yale University psychologist, has developed a test that evaluates creativity and problem solving rather than analytical skills alone that form the main, if not sole, focus of current scholastic tests (SAT). Sternberg's test, dubbed "The Rainbow Project," asks students to write captions, outline how they would solve a problem, or write stories with unusual titles like "The Octopus's Sneakers" or "35,381." What most interests many experts about this experimental testing is that it appears to predict first-year students' college performance (GPA — Grade Point Average) more accurately than do the SAT scores, and with a narrower gap between ethnic and socio-economic groups. Prof. Sternberg was seeking funding for an expanded trial that would show if the patterns hold beyond the initial 800-student sample.[15]

A study by Daniel Goleman in the mid-1990s, *Emotional Intelligence,* talks about emotions as a source of real intelligence. He refers to Peter Salovey of Yale who has described five main domains of emotional intelligence: knowing your emotions or self-awareness; self-management, handling feelings properly; motivating oneself, controlling impulsiveness; recognition of emotions in others; and handling relationships well. However, "schools and culture are fixated on academic ability…even though there is every indication that a higher IQ is no guarantee of prosperity, prestige, or happiness (i.e., success)…they ignore a more reliable guide (in stressing academic ability): emotional intelligence, a new concept but one which research suggests can be as powerful, and at times more powerful than IQ."[16]

In the light of research studies — such as the above done at renowned universities (of the *Ivy League)* — academic testing in the United States is being modified. Thus, the SAT conductors have expanded the *writing test* and have added an *essay.* Undoubtedly, there is a growing recognition that narrow testing of a purely academic type is not a satisfactory measure of one's abilities and potential to succeed in studies, a career, and in life, overall.

In talking about the above innovations, the idea is not to devalue the assessment of academic abilities for civil service examinations, but to consider including tests of *other determinants* of anticipated performance in the light of job requirements *in the Indian setting.* In particular, the tests should include the measurement of creative ability and adaptability/attitudinal flexibility. It has been found that extra-curricular proclivities and achievements and *street smarts* also happen to be important factors for success in many real life situations, which, at times, can become complex and tense. The selection criteria and the examination system should be scrutinized carefully to see how one could incorporate in the *expanded* testing methods (written, *impromptu* writing, performance in group discussions, and interview) these additional factors that seem to predict future performance. Ideally, the examination system should be tailored to suit the needs of different Services, as stated earlier. Some Papers could be common for all candidates but others should be designed to measure the abilities and traits needed in the specific Service; obviously, the needs for *auditing* are substantially different from those for *policing.* Some ideas on the subject of differentiated requirements are presented in the next section while dealing with the traits that would be helpful in a Foreign Service career.

Before moving to that section, it may be added that creating new Services recommended above is not intended to, and should not, result in a larger number of bureaucrats; already there are *far more* of them in the country than are required. In fact, the need is to reduce the number to cut back costs and, in many cases, to allow more elbowroom for functioning — for providing better public services. Currently, the input of labour seen in relation to the quantum and quality of output of our civil servants indicates a very low level of productivity.

Creation of additional civil services would really amount to a combination of name changes, reorganization, reassignments, etc., because technical people are already serving in the government; only that they are treated as second-class civil servants and are working at levels below their potential, their true worth, since the current setup does not harness their services productively in the cause of spurring development.

Some of the measures taken by the government over the years amount to an implicit recognition of the shortcomings of the present bureaucracy. These measures include mainly the devolution of powers to local self-government bodies, and giving funds to Members of Parliament (M.P.s) for carrying out developmental activities. Prime Minister Rajiv Gandhi was the originator of the idea. He had once told an assembly of collectors from all over the country that they were functioning as *democratic dictators.* He was, therefore, initiating the movement of functions of development to elected *panchayats* and other self-governing bodies. Prime Minister Narasimha Rao pushed the idea, persuading Parliament to pass the 73rd and 74th Amendments to the Constitution for devolution of the development authority to *panchayat-raj* bodies. Rao also introduced the scheme of assigning one crore rupees to each M.P. for development works in their areas; the amount was later raised to two crores.

Now there is a need to go a step further and give elected bodies the power to recruit staff that would be supervised and controlled by them — the sort of arrangement that is generally operating in democratic countries. Thus, in the United States local bodies' elected representatives run the county (district)/city government agencies. The local police and school administrations and other public service bodies are responsible to the county's elected Board of Supervisors, City Council, etc. As stated by Mani Shankar Aiyar: "A centralized bureaucracy is incompatible with a decentralized polity. In every real democracy in the world, local government is administered by locally recruited staff...Administration by the people, of the people, and for the people is the only way. Independence for the country can be translated, a half-century after 1947, into freedom for the people. The steel frame must be dismantled. And a bamboo frame erected in its place."[17]

Gradual but bold steps should be taken towards achieving development-oriented local self-government. Proper directions and training would be needed in the beginning but there is no reason why local self-government could not be achieved in due course with guidance, cooperation, and encouragement from the political leadership, bureaucracy, and the civil society at large.

V

MAKE BUREAUCRACY LESS INSULAR

The trodden path is the safest.

—Legal Maxim

Insularity, which creates a sense of safety and contentedness, is another problem facing India's civil services. One enters this fraternity at a relatively young age and usually remains there until retirement, working in set ways and dealing with each other in a somewhat closed environment suffused with elitism, especially in senior Services. Deputation to outside agencies and foreign assignments do help to broaden a bureaucrat's horizon; nonetheless, an insular, non-enterprising culture has developed. Outsiders normally are not admitted into the civil service at middle and senior levels. This lack of lateral entry of experts deprives the system of the talent of very competent people — technocrats and specialists — who have gathered valuable experience outside the ambit of civil services. Wouldn't a successful businessman, who has proper academic credentials and training, be an asset if co-opted by the bureaucracy for service in economic ministries? (They are taken in the public-sector undertakings at high levels.) And, why not consider a university vice-chancellor for the post of Secretary or another senior assignment in the ministry of education?

In the United States, a healthy interchange of people between the government, industry, and academia is encouraged — not only through political appointments (Presidential, Schedule C, etc.) but also through recruitment into career civil services at practically all levels. To cite an excellent example: A dean of the country's leading textile school — at N.C. State University at Raleigh — served earlier as a professor; then joined the federal government as an Assistant or Deputy Assistant Secretary; subsequently he moved to Monsanto Chemical Company as Vice President for synthetic textile fibers; and finally came back to N.C. State University as Dean of the textile school. He had left his mark in every position, bringing fresh ideas and *other ways* to look at things. His perspective widened and the snowballing experiences — in academia, in policy and administrative fields, and in industry — made him progressively more valuable.[1] In India, we have very limited opportunities of this kind — only through political appointments, which account for a miniscule proportion of the country's overall governance machinery.[2]

In civil services, *per se,* we have had a limited number of outside entrants — only at senior levels. It would be highly desirable to enable the system to induct many more outsiders in order to utilize their special backgrounds and talents. There are numerous very specialized jobs where outsiders — with proper credentials — would be highly useful, e.g., in trade negotiations. Arvind Panagaria talks about U.S. practices in this regard: "In the past decade, every U.S. Trade Representative has been a top trade lawyer. This is not surprising since lawyers are known to earn their living by negotiating on behalf of their clients. While we may lack such lawyers today, we must pave the way for their future emergence."[3] However, there are many areas where we do have individuals with extraordinary skills and knowledge who can, and should, be brought into the government as senior civil servants (as had happened, say, with Montek Singh Ahluwalia, who served as Secretary to the Government of India in economic ministries); as bureaucrats they could be offered short/medium-term contract jobs or absorbed in the regular bureaucracy.

Some increase in the number of political appointments of specialists should also be considered — for new positions falling between the ministers and the topmost tier of civil services. This would mean creating some positions and/or converting certain senior civil service positions in cases where specialized knowledge or experience is needed and/or the policy content of job responsibilities is relatively high. The appointees to these new political positions would not be considered civil servants. This would resemble the U.S. system where the number of political appointees is large — unduly so according to some public administration experts. Going part ways in that direction would be helpful, as it would attract competent, successful people to work in specialized areas. They would be the type of individuals who do not wish to become regular civil servants but are willing to engage in public service for short periods — concurrent with the term of ministers and most political appointees. However, all such recruitment to senior civil service levels, or to expanded political jobs, should be done according to proper procedures. Political calculations, manipulations, and cronyism should be checked firmly to ensure merit-based hiring and to preserve the integrity of the administrative and policy-making infrastructure.

A couple of senior civil servants with whom the induction of outsiders into the government at senior levels was discussed expressed a bit of concern about the handling of classified, secret/top-secret material by *short-term* appointees after they leave office. Supposing some of them decided to use confidential information to pen books/articles, of 'spilling-the-beans' or 'kiss-and-tell' type?[4] The concern is genuine — not entirely without foundation judging from some known cases of breach of confidentiality trust committed by short-term political appointees as well as by regular bureaucrats, not only in India but other countries also. Thus, one of the senior-most security officials in the U.S. — Sandy Berger, the President's National Security Adviser, of all people — admitted to having taken some highly classified, sensitive material from the National Archives! This points to the necessity of taking all due precautions to ensure confidentiality/safekeeping of all secret material by short-term appointees — through official, legal stipulations, including clearance and embargo requirements, and necessary orientation for them regarding confidentiality procedures and statutes. The requirements should also be strengthened for regular bureaucrats and others associated with the government (e.g., consultants handling sensitive material), wherever found necessary.

While making a case for outsiders getting entry into civil services, one should not be oblivious to the fact that civil servants, too, deserve to be provided opportunities to work outside — in the universities, think tanks, public corporations, etc. This is important in the context of widening their horizons of thinking and creativity. They will be richer for the experience and will return to the government with fresher, newer ideas.[5] And, by the same token, they will contribute to the enrichment of the experience of those working with these civil servants who would be bringing a somewhat different perspective to the mix. The result, a cross-pollination of ideas and practices, would undoubtedly lead to the ultimate betterment of the nation's governance. However, while sending bureaucrats for gaining outside experience, the government will have to ensure —through bond undertaking or other binding measures — that at least a significant proportion of them return to their cadres.[6]

Based on the author's experience, it seems that the two-way traffic between groups of civil servants and outside experts would be particularly useful in the area of foreign affairs. A think-tanker, for instance, could undertake valuable work on long-term diplomatic strategies and perspective planning in the External Affairs Ministry at New Delhi. And, similarly, a diplomat with extensive experience in a region, say South Asia, would be well-placed to conduct research, and teach, at a university or institute where such work (area studies) is being carried out. A limited amount of movement of this type is, in fact, occurring but much more needs to be done.

Regarding political appointments of specialists, recent years have seen cases where seemingly improper appointments have unfortunately been made for posts of an analytical/policy-formulating nature — e.g., of practicing politicians in the Planning Commission. Members of the Planning Commission have usually been — invariably in earlier decades — people of outstanding academic achievements, including world-class economists/agricultural economists like Professors V.K.R.V. Rao, Raj Krishna, A.M. Khusro, J.D. Sethi, A. Vaidyanathan, and Yogendra Alagh (the author's immediate predecessor as Member i/c Agriculture), or reputed scientists like Professors M.S. Swaminathan and P.N. Srivastava. A large number of members had been, or later became, vice-chancellors. By contrast, a few appointments have lately been made — apparently on purely political considerations. Some of them did not seem to possess even the basic qualifications and minimum academic credentials in the field of their specialization — forget advanced degrees or adequate research/analytical experience for handling significant and intricate policy issues. Can't we preserve at least *a few* areas for academicians where they are *needed* and can make meaningful contributions? As such, not many high-level positions are available to them and most of these intellectuals — due to the nature of their work and deportment — are not good at pulling strings and managing to land even policy-making jobs for which they have the *best* credentials. Usually, the leaders have to seek them out. This is in sharp contrast to the case of politically savvy people who know when to lobby, where to put political pressure, and how to go all out to get important appointments; their suitability for the posts in question does not appear to be a terribly relevant consideration — at least not for them! Resort to *jugad* technology and getting *some* important post — preferably one that enables them to stay in a ministerial or other government bungalow in New Delhi's "Green/Emerald Zone" — is all that seems to matter for them!

One objection raised against the proposal to induct some outsiders into the civil service at upper levels is that even a limited influx would unfavourably affect the fortunes of existing bureaucrats, especially by limiting their promotional opportunities. That would, of course, be true but the situation could be handled through some protective measures: For the *short-run,* safeguard the interests of existing bureaucrats by ensuring pay protection; giving promotion in place (with no basic change in responsibilities) *a la'* the system in universities. There, for example, an associate professor after serving for a fixed number of years may be given a *personal promotion* to full professorship even though he/she may continue to do the same work as was being performed earlier as an associate professor. Also, opportunities could be found elsewhere, e.g., in the public sector, and other creative solutions sought. Bureaucrats entered civil services anticipating career paths indicated in their service conditions and in line with past traditions and, in all fairness, that compact with them should be honoured.

For the *long-run,* the solution is simple: reduce the size of the intake in keeping with the reduction in the size of some Services and in promotional opportunities consequent upon the induction of outsiders at middle and senior levels of bureaucracy.

VI

INDUCT MORE OUTSIDERS INTO THE FOREIGN SERVICE

All things must change
To something new
To something strange.

—Longfellow

Outside entrants at upper-middle and senior levels would be very helpful in India's Foreign Service. At the moment, there are only a miniscule number of politically appointed diplomats. Many countries have a much larger proportion of such appointees, e.g. the United States. In Pakistan, the ratio is even higher, at one time a substantial number of diplomats were from outside the Foreign Service; they had been senior retired/serving military officers, political leaders, noted public figures, and others — including feudal lords.[1]

Properly chosen outsiders can perform well and, in fact, past appointees generally have had a commendable record. Wider experience of the right type cannot but help an ambassador. It all depends upon the choices made by the government — often by the Prime Minister himself for key postings. The government should, of course, follow proper norms in making such appointments: *Political appointments do not have to be made on political considerations.*

Personally — as a politically appointed ambassador — the author found his earlier, varied experiences very helpful. One specific instance relates to arranging a very successful State visit to India by the President of Maldives, H.E. Maumoon Abdul Gayoom. It was considered more desirable to arrange a trip to a place other than the oft-visited tourist cities (like Agra and Jaipur), of course, in addition to Delhi. In any case, this president had visited such tourist destinations more than once. The out-of-way Pondicherry was suggested. It is an attractive city in the author's not-unbiased opinion; it is scenic and a historic cultural and educational centre, and home of the famed Aurobindo *Ashram.* It was arranged that Pondicherry Central University would confer an honorary doctorate on President Gayoom. Besides the usual official programs at Delhi, which were impressive, a meeting (in a symposium format) was fixed in a parliament annex auditorium, which was attended by some top environmentalists of the country. The address by the Maldivian President, an authority on the subject of environment (especially global warming), was very well received. All of the substantive program of the president and his entourage was developed in the Mission at Malé and it was possible because of the ambassador's earlier stints as a university vice-chancellor, in the Planning Commission at Delhi, and at Pondicherry, and his very close contacts with environmental experts. Thus, the meeting in the parliament complex was arranged with help from Anil Agrawal and Sunita Narain (Director and Deputy Director, respectively, of the Centre for Science and Environment, CSE) who were close friends of the ambassador and had been fellow attendees with him at the Rio Earth Summit in 1992 — Anil as an official delegate and Sunita as a representative of CSE. They had also visited Maldives twice to pursue the common interest — the country's environmental problems.

It is not the contention here that a career IFS ambassador would not be able to do this, for they do it all the time, and creditably. The point merely is that the author's earlier positions and interests made it more convenient to arrange an above-average, interesting, and useful program expeditiously. Moreover, knowing well the main actors in the arrangements at Delhi and Pondicherry added personal touch to the warmth and hospitality extended to the Maldivian President, the First Lady, and members of the visiting delegation.

There are a number of qualified people outside the Foreign Service who would make excellent diplomats and the government should consider inducting some of them — as recommended for entry in other civil services. Distinguished academics, experts in the fields of international studies[2], talented politicians, especially those who have handled foreign relations[3], and others who have already made a name in their vocations constitute an excellent pool of potential appointees.[4] In fact, Prime Minister Nehru had tapped *many* outsiders to serve as ambassadors — especially during the early post-Independence period — including Dr. S. Radhakrishnan (future President of India) to the USSR; V.K. Krishna Menon to the U.K.;

Sardar K.M. Panikkar to China; Vijay Lakshmi Pandit to the United States; B.N. Rau to the United Nations; Ali Yavar Jung to Egypt (he also served later as ambassador to the United States); G. Parthasarathy to Pakistan; Apa Pant to Kenya; and some others. Some people were also taken from the Princely States — into the regular IFS and as political appointees at senior levels. All of these outsiders generally performed their duties well, most of them superbly.

However, the recruitment of outsiders should be done in a way that does not adversely affect the prospects of regular members of the IFS. Reducing the Foreign Service intake, and taking some additional measures — as indicated for other civil services — should be able to satisfy the requirements of fairness towards members of the IFS and meet wider equity considerations.

In diplomatic posts where specialized knowledge is required — or is highly desirable — outside appointees could sometimes fit the bill very well. Thus, in Rome, where the Mission takes care of representation at the U.N. Food and Agriculture Organization (FAO), posting an agricultural policy expert — with other relevant experience — would be ideal, as ambassador/minister/counsellor.[5] The same holds true for Geneva and Brussels embassies that handle a lot of economic matters (representation at WTO and EEC) where economic policy/trade experts would be able to protect India's interests while contributing to the solution of global economic problems. However, no particular post, or total number of ex-cadre appointments, should be treated as *reserved* for outsiders; decisions should be taken on a case-by-case consideration of suitable appointees in the light of potential "value addition" and the government's requirements at the time.

So far as the selection of regular IFS entrants is concerned, the process should take into account special job requirements, and emphasize traits that a good diplomat ought to possess. The author had put in many years in this area — as an international civil servant for over two decades and as an envoy for India for one extended term — and observed closely some of the desirable characteristics that good diplomats displayed; these appeared as second nature in the case of highly successful ambassadors and others engaged in international affairs, and especially came to the fore during emergencies or sticky situations. *Good communication skills, sociability*[6], and *multicultural orientation* certainly are three basic traits needed for people in the diplomatic corps (these would also serve other civil servants well). Written examinations and interviews should, therefore, be geared to assess these qualities. At the moment, the tests for the IFS, IAS, and Allied Services are more or less the same and the qualifying candidates who score the highest total marks are offered the IFS, and then IAS, followed by other Services. There are certain clear-cut differences in responsibilities, work environment, and locale, etc. (e.g. between a diplomat and an Accounts and Audit Service officer), that are not taken into account in the selection process; the approach seems to be: select an *all-purpose* civil servant. The recruiters believe that *one size would fit all!*

In the United States, recruitment to the Foreign Service is handled by the State Department (External Affairs Ministry) itself; there is no all-U.S. civil service similar to the IAS and Allied Services. The process for the selection of the U.S. Foreign Service Officers (FSOs) is briefly described here.[7] The department looks for qualities that make successful FSOs — persuasive skills, reasoning and analysis, and how well one works with others. It also helps if one speaks a foreign language or two. The testing is rigorous. To succeed, applicants really have to ask themselves some pertinent questions before taking the tests: Am I interested in public service? Can I forgo creature comforts? Can I write well and fast? Do I pick up foreign languages easily? Do I have a sense of adventure?

In 2004, about 19,100 took the written examination — the first step. Those who passed (some 4,400) were tested further — for a whole day. They showed up at 7 a.m. and, after introductions, got to reading a selected, important book. They were allowed 30 minutes to *prepare a briefing,* and got 6 minutes to *present their case.* Then, *as a group*, they spent about 60 minutes to *find a consensus approach* on the issue(s) covered in the book. There was also a 90-minute exercise — *writing a memo* for the boss — and an *interview,* to give candidates a chance to explain their positions and to assess their motivations through a series of questions. The day of the testing, over by 6 p.m. or so, leads to a winnowing down of the number of aspirants (to between 600 and 750); their names are then placed on a register for hiring, according to the scores on various tests. Of them — after some further whittling down on the basis of medical tests and security considerations — upward of 400 Foreign Service Officers were to be hired; the intake was expected to continue at this level for the next few years prompted in part by post-9/11 demands and the Secretary of State's *diplomatic readiness initiative.*

Recruitment procedures in many private American companies appear even more innovative in some respects than in U.S. civil services.[8] The famous Universal Studios Hollywood, for instance, administers *advanced personality tests* to potential employees even at relatively low job levels. Applicants first take a 50-minute online test (on a computer) containing questions, answers to which would tell a lot about their personalities. The tests are tough: Out of more than 20,000 applicants tested in 2004, the company hired only around 1,900, which represents an admission rate lower than that for Harvard University. The tests for Universal Studios Hollywood were developed by Unicru Inc., a leader in the employment testing industry.

Over the past few years personality tests have moved from the realm of experiments to standard practice at many of the largest American companies, including luxury retailers like Neiman Marcus, and large store chains such as Target and Albertson's (grocery stores). A high proportion of U.S. companies are now using personality tests in hiring and they regard such tests as important as — if not more important than — an applicant's education, experience, and recommendations. The main personality assessment tests include the *Myers-Briggs Type Indicator,* which measures four qualities of a person: introversion/extroversion, sensing/intuition, thinking/feeling, judging/perceiving, and is often used to help match people with careers. The *Minnesota Multiphasic Personality Inventory,* which attempts to measure behavioural propensities for substance abuse to serious pathologies, is regularly used to assess candidates for sensitive positions in police departments, banks, nuclear plants, and the like. *The Neuroticism, Extroversion and Openness Personality Inventory* (NEO-PI) breaks personality down into five characteristics that some companies use to assess traits such as the management potential. Today an estimated 2,500 U.S. companies offer assessments that are mostly variations of these main tests and are geared towards hiring.

Tests like the ones described above can be excellent selection tools for identifying people with different personality traits and matching them with particular jobs requiring those very traits. However, since such tests do not yield definitive and complete results, they should be treated only as a part of overall assessment procedures which should include in addition: written examination(s); group discussions; and individual and group interviews, etc.

One should examine carefully the U.S. models for recruitment and also models used in some other countries to see what would suit

India's requirements and socio-cultural imperatives. The procedures should ultimately reflect the needs and traditions of the country, seen in the light of long-term foreign policy objectives, including, of course, the push towards claiming an important, rightful place in the global arena.

The reforms needed in the Indian Foreign Service would be of a somewhat different nature than in other civil services because of the obvious differences in goals and responsibilities of diplomatic personnel and their work environment. According to Kishen S. Rana, a retired senior diplomat, reforms are long overdue: "Although all but one of the foreign ministries of the 19 countries of the E.U. and G-8 have carried out structural changes since 1990 to cope with changes in the post-Cold War world (according to a comparative study by the Italian Foreign Ministry), MEA (India's Ministry of External Affairs) has so far limited itself to handle relations with the strategically important Central Asian countries. Deeper structural change has yet to materialize, though some reforms are under consideration."[9] Two such structural reform measures relate to the creation of a Foreign Service Inspectorate (vital to undertake periodic inspection of all missions, ensure uniformity of standards, and help to enhance their performance) and placement of IFS officials within the administration of some states to help in the area of international contacts.

Rana also refers to lack of creative foreign policy thinking in the context of regional considerations: "In regional diplomacy, being adept at tactics is not enough when policy has been unimaginative or defensive. This has been the case, for example, in India's past stance *vis-à-vis* ASEAN, when opportunities for close association were passed up in the 1980s."[10] Defensiveness seems also to have crippled India's approach to the South Asian Association for Regional Cooperation (SAARC), where a fear of all the smaller neighbours ganging up has blocked innovative ideas to overcome the impasse created by Pakistan's obduracy.

Our foreign policy analysis is weak and long-term planning even weaker. To take an example, there is no formal analysis of the cost-benefit ratio for India's foreign assistance projects — either *intra-country* (projects within a country) or *inter-country* (between countries). Should we establish a big hospital in Maldives' capital, Male′, or small clinics in individual, far-flung islands, or set up educational institutions and specialized vocational training centers?

The country did not have any such educational facilities beyond the High School level as of mid-1990s. Or, would a hospital in Nepal or Zambia give better returns in terms of meeting felt needs and generating goodwill? While measuring these returns could never be a rigorous exercise in statistical terms, and subjective criteria would definitely enter in the equation, some objectivity can certainly be introduced before large aid commitments are made. Decisions have been taken in the past by the Prime Minister, the External Affairs Minister, and senior officers in the MEA without a satisfactory analysis of needs, absorptive capacity of the recipient country, or better alternative uses for the assistance funding that a country like India can spare at its present stage of development.

Another area needing considerable improvement relates to in-house training of personnel. The facilities at the External Affairs Ministry's Foreign Service Institute are inadequate in terms of coverage as well as quality of instruction.

It may be added here that in many countries think tanks and universities conduct a significant amount of analysis of important foreign policy issues and make projections of future scenarios based on in-house research as well as use of outside information, both quantitative and qualitative. Such work provides excellent input to the administration. To illustrate, in the United States valuable material coming from some leading universities (e.g. Johns Hopkins University's School for Advanced International Studies) and think tanks (the Brookings Institution, Woodrow Wilson International Center for Scholars, Center for Strategic and International Studies, and numerous others located in Washington, D.C.) is supplemented by the outstanding work done in many areas by the U.S. Congress — in the House and Senate Committees dealing with international affairs and by the Congressional Research Service. This work by the legislative wing of government and by academic centers appears to have, on many issues, swayed foreign policy decisions more than has the policy output generated within the administration (the State Department, various intelligence agencies, and other government offices).

Obviously, there is need in India to set up more, independent think tanks; encourage better-quality research in academic institutions; and to upgrade the activities of the existing non-government groups for the purpose of receiving independent foreign policy advice to supplement the information available within the government.

Of course, the above comments also apply to the domestic policy sector where outside agencies can study various important issues and offer valuable advice to the concerned ministries and other offices. In general, there is considerable scope in India to strengthen non-government study and/or action centres and other civil society groups, which would undoubtedly lead to the enrichment of our practice of democracy.

To conclude this chapter, Rana's observation in the Paper referred to earlier — that our Foreign Service possesses "the latent capacity to perform far better, provided that real reform can be implemented in the MEA and its processes"[11] — is shared widely in international circles. The quality of our diplomatic people can be judged, for instance, by the usually better than average — often outstanding — performance of Indian diplomats at international gatherings or of those seconded to international (inter-governmental or quasi-governmental) organizations.

VII

BANISH ELITISM FROM BUREAUCRACY

The administrative structure you have [in India] is a colonial legacy designed to serve an imperial power...The system is based on the principle that the government owns the people. That's antithetical to India's otherwise vibrant democracy. People should own the government, not the other way round.

— *Mark Tully*[1]

Elitism in civil services remains a serious problem despite efforts at democratization, especially expansion in the powers of local self-government entities and development of civil society with an increasing — but still rather limited — role played by non-government organizations (NGOs). Elitism persists because of, among other things, the centralization of power with officials at many levels — Centre, state, and the district. That our civil service is a legacy of the British rule is, of course, apparent to people in India. According to V. Sundaram, a senior member of the IAS, "Our system and structures of public administration — relics of a colonial past — still continue almost intact...The system does not hear enough from those who suffer on account of it. The common people of India are treated all the time like consumables in the system."[2]

However, the commonalities between the present civil services and the imperial administrative structure of the Raj period — generalist, all-purpose cadre oriented towards administration and control and not development and welfare; elitism, hauteur, and aloofness displayed by bureaucrats and lack of accountability, especially to the public — are, for obvious reasons, strikingly obvious to British journalists and other foreign observers of the Indian scene. Besides Mark Tully of the BBC (quoted above), Edward Luce, another Englishman who knows India well (worked for *The Financial Times* and is married to an Indian) has commented on the phenomenon in a book that came out only some months ago; it contains a longish chapter on Indian bureaucracy, "The Burra Sahibs: The Long Tentacles of India's State." Luce states, "the chief influence that continues to shape India's state today is British — with some lingering traces of the Mughals. Remote from the people and Olympian in its self-image, the British colonial administration...left a tradition of detachment and paternalism that remains evident today...I have visited many of the colonial whitewashed bungalows inhabited by district collectors across India and wandered into numerous district 'collectorates' — the local headquarters where the official presides both as the local magistrate and as the local arm of the executive. Although the portrait hanging in the collector's office is of Mohandas Gandhi rather than King George IV, a nineteenth century British colonial official would feel immediately at home. The collector is surrounded by a beehive of peons and never moves anywhere within the district without a phalanx of sidekicks. At every village he (or increasingly she) will be garlanded like a film star with carnations, jasmines or marigolds...Even the collector's mode of transport, a colonial-era white Ambassador with an insistent red light flashing on top, is unchanged from the later days of the Raj."[3,4] The sense of privilege and a degree of grandeur sometimes (fortunately, only rarely) leads to bizarre expression of power by an errant bureaucrat.[5]

Surprisingly, even today, the district collector controls a lot, wielding much more power than any, or extremely low number of, democratic societies actually permit or should permit. To quote Edward Luce again: "The legacy of Nehru's Englishness...is visible in every corner of early twenty-first-century India, in the little-altered system of district collectors...[Their cadre, IAS, is] staffed by an unsackable elite, for whom democracy is something of a rival...[There is] uneasy, at times bizarre relationship between the IAS and India's elected but often semi-literate provincial leaders.[6]

The power of the collector can be gauged from the fact that he/she writes — or has important input in — the performance reports (annual confidential report, ACR) of all, or most, of the senior officers, including the Indian Police Service officers. This used to be the case in Haryana, and presumably in numerous other states a few years ago.[7] Why should a collector write the ACRs of the chief medical officer, the district engineer, or the senior superintendent of police? Couldn't their supervisors — regional medical officers, superintending engineers, and deputy inspectors general of police —

write ACRs of their own officers?[8] After all, they are more knowledgeable than the collector about the activities of their charges and possess the competence to assess their performance.[9]

It's time that India's governance — now *of* the people and *for* the people (still with some acknowledged faults) is also made *by* the people, through devolution of power to the local self-government bodies. The office of the collector could be kept for some time but the incumbent should be treated as the *coordinator* of district level activities, not the *boss,* in order to reduce elitism. That would be fair and would also make sense in terms of functional efficiency; eliminate inter-service tensions; and improve the overall morale of the bureaucracy. The powers of the elected local-self-government representatives should be increased in tandem with the steps to reduce the authority of the collector. This would be in keeping with the governance structures in democratic countries, particularly the developed ones. Thus, in the United States, who runs the county (district) administration? Certainly not a collector like bureaucrat, but *an elected board of supervisors and a chairman elected directly or chosen by board members.* The county police, the school system, and all paid functionaries are ultimately responsible to the elected officials of the county.

One cannot deny that corruption is also very much there in India's local self-government bodies at the district and sub-district levels — from district boards, block committees, down to the village *panchayats* (councils); references have been made elsewhere to political corruption in general. So, why suggest giving more powers to elected representatives? Because *that's the essence of democratic functioning* — there is no other way in a free society. Devolution of power to local levels should be the *mantra.* Fortunately, steps have already been taken in this direction. Of course, we have to reform the political system as a whole but that is a complex subject needing a detailed, expert analysis.

Coming back to elitism, another contributor to it — in addition to the centralization of powers — is giving undue perks and high visibility to civil servants, such as big houses (old residences of collectors, who usually finish the district assignments within the first seven to ten years of service, are on huge lots); cars with red/blue lights on top; gunmen (now they accompany even some of the second-rung district/sub-divisional officials!); big offices; large staff including domestic help; and so on. Looking at such ostentatious life style, anyone — and not just British and other foreign observers — would rightly conclude that the colonial-era British system created by Mill and Metcalfe has not changed all that much; only that now we have *brown sahibs* as the new guardians![10] Some of the undesirable social traits (undue deference to authority, lingering sycophancy, and residual feudalism in some areas), of course, also contribute to the maintenance of elitism. Whatever the causes, the situation is patently incongruous in a democracy.

Regarding the ways of the bureaucrats, Tavleen Singh feels strongly that "the vanity of our officials has to be curbed." She, too, is irked by the undue and showy perks of the bureaucrats in the districts, where "Collectors live like potentates in mighty mansions whose high walls ensured that they got never a glimpse of the people they were meant to serve." She reminds us that even Jawahar Lal Nehru, the creator of a nanny state, had admitted at the end of his years that "one of his biggest mistakes was to trust the bureaucracy to implement his dreams." The time has come according to Tavleen Singh "to abolish the permanent civil service and start hiring people on contracts renewable every five years. This already happens in some countries."[11] The idea to hire bureaucrats on short-term contracts — raised elsewhere in this book — is sensible and timely. However, a small core of civil service should comprise regular employees who will make it a career and provide continuity and stability needed for parts of the civil service structure.

Before Wajahat Habibullah, a senior member of the IAS, left the U.S. a few years ago[12], the author had a conversation with him on the subject of Indian bureaucracy and the need for reforms. One of his important points also related to the issue of removing elitism in civil services. He had tried to convey the message to probationer trainees at the Lal Bahadur Shastri Academy of Administration at Mussorie (when he was director of that institute) that elitism and democracy do not go together. That spirit guided his own conduct; among other meaningful gestures, he was able to persuade the government to remove the red light from the top of his car.

At times, elitism and arrogance make civil servants do unnecessary things to show their importance — e.g. providing guard-of-honour to mid-level bureaucrats![13] In stark contrast, the governors (who, like others in the category of 'very very important persons,' VVIPs, are extended the honour) have been cutting down on the practice.[14] It may be added that an individual — if not very careful — can easily get used to some of the privileges and perks, and feel elated at the obeisance. Once, when asked about the subject, President John F. Kennedy of the United States — a truly democratic society — had said that when *Hail to the Chief* was played he did feel *special, exalted* (or words to that effect)![15]

One important way to reduce elitism in civil services would be to modify the hierarchical structure. Lower ranking officers should be allowed to go up to levels higher than they reach at present. That would also lead to better administration. We will have the benefit of the experience of such officers at the level of public dealing or being street savvy — say "practical policing" in the case of law and order personnel. Ved Marwah, IPS (an ex-governor, and a noted think tanker) maintains: "There is no substitute for experience. IPS officers cannot afford to be *sahibs* and need to justify their seniority by being hard-boiled professionals. Ideally, every IPS officer must rise from the lowest rank possible, even as a constable, as it is the constable who interacts most with the public. This is prevalent in western countries where there is no rigid hierarchy between the senior supervisory officers and the rank and file in the police force.[16] Homogenization is necessary to reduce the alienation that the lower rank policeman experiences with his superiors who do not appreciate his difficulties.[17] Accelerated promotions may be given to educated and deserving officers, but all must have thorough experience of work at the lower levels. It is only then that senior officers will be able to guide their subordinates, thereby easing their work, and not give impossible orders as they are often accused of doing."[18] This suggestion — generally applicable to other Services as well — would certainly result in reduced elitism in addition to improved efficiency.

At present a sub-inspector of police (entering the service usually after a bachelor's or even master's degree) does not normally go beyond two levels — the ranks of inspector and deputy superintendent (Dy. S.P.). Aren't there some among them who would make a good superintendent of police (S.P.) or even deputy inspector general (D.I.G.)? The same is true of the army. The recruit (many are now enlisting after undergraduate degrees if not higher, because of a lack of employment opportunities), unless selected for receiving a commission early in his/her service career, can only aspire to go to the highest rank of a subedar/risaldar major. This category of junior officers and that of the commissioned officers (who start as 2nd lieutenants) do not intersect at all.

Members of State Services (PCS, PPS, etc.) often complain about being shut out from many senior, desirable positions even after their promotion to All-India Services — IAS, IPS, and others. In 1996, Prime Minister H.D. Deve Gowda (who also held the charge of the personnel ministry) had made/blessed a suggestion to slash direct recruitment to the IAS, IPS, and the Indian Forest Service over the coming five years and increase the quota for promotion from respective state civil services to the all-India cadres. Such a cadre management policy, if adopted, will have a significant bearing on the federal administrative structure, as more officers from state civil services will be able to reach top positions.[19]

Due to the frustration long felt by them, the Union Territory (UT) officers of the Delhi, Andaman & Nicobar Islands Civil Service (DANICS), mounted an agitation in 1996. They represented their case to the Delhi Chief Minister and the Chief Secretary, stating that while Delhi UT had 35 sanctioned posts for the IAS, there were about 70 to 80 officers posted in the UT; the surplus officers are accommodated in the ex-cadre posts in various civic bodies. The DANICS officers would like their share of ex-cadre posts, which would resolve, at least partially, the problem of stagnation and also boost the sagging morale of these officers. The DANICS representation asked: "How long can one play second fiddle? After all, we have also been recruited through the same selection process as the IAS officers."[20]

In closing this section, the author wishes to quote one of friends, Anadi Naik, who is now living in the United States. He was a dedicated social worker in India in his younger days and had also worked in Vinoba Bhave's *Bhoodan* movement and is thus irked — much more than most people — by our bureaucracy's attitude: "The mindset of the individual bureaucrat has always been to create an aura of self-importance. The needs of the people, whose tax money pays the salary of the bureaucrat, takes a back seat in his/her thinking process...The more experienced a government employee grows in his /her job, the more obstructionist and corrupt he/she seems to become...No country can afford to tolerate a situation like this."[21]

VIII

INTRODUCE GREATER ACCOUNTABILITY IN CIVIL SERVICES

The perfect bureaucrat everywhere is the man who manages to make no decisions and escape all responsibility.

—Brooks Atkinson

The accountability concept and practice are very weak in Indian bureaucracy. There is nearly perfect security of tenure, promotions are time-bound, and no — or not much — punishment is ever meted out for inefficiency, irresponsibility, or misconduct. Some civil servants maintain, in a lighter vein, that IAS stands for *"I Am Safe"!* But forget the senior Services, the government can hardly fire a peon!

There are basically good individuals in our civil services but the system as a whole has become such that efficiency, the sense of responsibility, and initiative are neither recognized nor rewarded, and favouritism, nepotism, and corruption have assumed cancerous proportions. The situation can only be remedied through forceful measures, including the following, to ensure accountability:

- Setting better standards to measure output and conduct of bureaucrats *annually,* and following the procedures meticulously.
- Rigorous rating of performance *at certain intervals* (say at 5, 10, and 15 years of service) that would determine promotion to higher levels and the type of assignments offered.[1] As of now, almost all Indian bureaucrats — and especially the members of the IAS and Allied services — are guaranteed upward movement and escalating emoluments unless there are really grave charges of corruption, or gross misconduct; inefficiency seems to be no bar to promotion.

- Reviewing and reforming bureaucratic systems periodically. Other countries undertake reforms from time to time to make their bureaucracies more efficient and accountable. In the United States, for instance, late 2003 saw an overhaul of the pay and personnel rules for 746,000 civil service employees of the Defense Department. In the previous year, the Department of Homeland Security was allowed to write pay and workplace rules for its 180,000 employees. This means that *more than half* of the U.S. federal workforce will no longer be anchored by civil service law. The evaluation and pay-scale framework has been changed significantly in these two big departments. Now their pay raises — both the timing and amount — will be linked to individual job performance and not to automatic annual pay raises in a pre-set scale. Employees also have less job protection and can be fired with less difficulty for non-performance and improper conduct, under the streamlined processes for disciplinary action, union negotiations, and resolution of labour disputes. Other government agencies are also contemplating changes.[2] For India, however, we cannot go quite that far at this time. Giving that much power and discretion to senior bosses would likely be misused in many cases due to the prevailing favouritism, cronyism, and an unacceptable level of general corruption.
- Guaranteeing consumer rights. As ill-luck would have it, consumer service is an alien concept for Indian bureaucrats. A customer seeking service should feel happy if he is not treated with discourtesy — and, at times, with contempt — in a government office, especially at district and lower levels. Customers have no rights and the service provided, if any, is a favour and not an entitlement! What is currently shown on an Indian TV channel — *Office Office* — is certainly realistic, though exaggerated at times for effect and for fun. It is, therefore, a very pleasant feeling when in other countries — mainly developed, but also in a number of developing ones — an official says: "Hello, may I help you," or "What can I do for you?" In the United States, it was no surprise to read the following in the *Business Week* magazine: "Who w'd have guessed the Social Security (a U.S. government office) folks give better customer service on the phone than Corporate America's role models."[3]

- Believing in "Putting Consumer First," almost all U.S. federal agencies have set *Customer Service Standards,* developed after consulting their customers. The standards are specific, not vague ("Lobby service in five minutes"). They are personalized and aim to meet customers' expectations. ("We will respond to your application within one business day.") They make firm commitments ("You'll only have to make one stop."), and so on. And, they provide specific avenues for complaints. ("If you have a problem...you may contact our Problem Resolution Office.")[4] It happens because the customer is important in the U.S., in other developed countries, and even in many developing countries.
- Reducing paper work. Cutting down administrative requirements and streamlining of procedures is urgently needed. For instance, the illogical government directive for submission of Life Certificate for a past period (attesting to the fact that you were really alive then also) is certainly annoying even though it has its funny side! It actually happened to the author in the mid-1960s in connection with two pension-like army awards granted originally to his father, good for two/three generations.[5] It must have been situations like this that prompted Will Rogers, the famous U.S. humorist, to say: "I don't make jokes; I just watch the government and report the facts."[6]

Rigid rules and illogical procedures have been curses indeed for a very long time, making people "go mad with fixed rule and method." (Horace, *Satires,* II, iii, 271.)

Upon returning to India in 1987 after working for 22 years in the United States as an international civil servant, the author was shocked to see the amount of paper work going on even in a university (CCS-Haryana Agricultural University). One felt suffocation looking at the files filling not only the big almirahs but also piling up on the top! Among many initiatives taken to reduce paper work and cut red-tapism, the practice of giving many verbal orders was started. "The vice-chancellor's word should be good enough but get written confirmation when necessary[7]; however, do not wait to act," were the instructions. For recording minutes of routine meetings it was decreed to note just the decisions rather than writing in detail who said what. These steps did reduce paper work significantly in some areas. Also, the frequency of the meetings was reduced as it was found that some of the issues could be easily settled on the telephone or in an informal get-together if the key parties involved were only two or three.

While rereading sections of Dharma Vira's autobiography during the preparation of this book, the author was glad to note that Akbar Hydari, ICS, a Departmental Secretary at Delhi *often* gave verbal orders. To quote from the book: "Akbar Hydari (later a Governor of Assam)...was a remarkable Secretary to work under. He was action-oriented and did not believe in long and learned notings on files. His method of work was to call the officers, discuss the files with them, and pass orders immediately. This method resulted in very quick disposal of work."[8]

J.M. Lobo Prabhu, another competent civil servant, also had a solution for expeditious disposal of files: "I made it a rule never to go to bed until I had disposed of the files sent from office. This had its salutary effect on the staff, to which I brought a system I had devised, that any paper not moved within a week should be signed in red ink — something that had a pronounced effect in checking delays."[9]

Even revising outdated forms can result in considerable reduction in paper work. Robert Chambers gives a telling example of obsolete information in official forms. The international driving permit issued to him by the Andhra Pradesh Government in 1980 listed non-existing countries and territories, e.g. Saar Territory — annexed by Hitler in 1935 — and French India. To the duplicated list of countries, U.S.A. and Canada had been added but, it seems, no countries were deleted or names updated. Chambers thought the effect could be maddening, or for the antiquarian, an intriguing delight![10] While the humour in such a situation — *a comedy of errors* — is delightful, the end result in many cases may not be benign and could, at times, cause much grief.

A century ago, Lord Curzon, Viceroy of India (1899–1905), too, was tormented by office procedures and practices: "Regular delay in office attendance, slow movement of files, uncalled-for lengthy noting on files, writing long minutes in flamboyant style, endless and purposeless movement of files up and down the desks, taking the stereotype as the model, dependence on subordinates for even a trifling matter."[11] Unfortunately, the situation has not changed much, except for the fact that writing is not so flamboyant or elegant these days.

Most people — based on personal experiences, as part of the long-suffering public or as pampered cogs in the administrative machinery — can unhesitatingly attest to the continuing presence of tormenting bureaucratic procedures and practices.

The subject of government files and slow decisions was the topic of a talk by Arun Shourie, the then Minister for Disinvestment, Communications, and IT, who cited an example of lack of decision making: "The residence of a high functionary of government is a splendid property. A tree fell on it nine years ago. The place remains unoccupied to this day…[is now] a *"bhoot bangla"* [ghost bungalow]. For nine years, officials have been exercising their minds on how and what repairs have to be carried out. A typical debate that has ranged in the files: some rule says that the residence of a functionary of that standing should be 760 sq. metres or less; the plan made by the architect turned out to be 780 sq. metres; sorting that wiggle took four months…and in the meantime, government pays Rupees 650,000 as rent every month for the alternative accommodation."[12]

Shourie talks elsewhere about another interesting case — really a farcical matter dealing with the issue whether (and when) civil servants should be permitted to use green ink, or red, in addition to the usual black/blue ink used to make notes on files/documents. The issue, which was resolved in almost one year, took a noticeable amount of time of some very senior officers in an inter-ministry exercise. The outcome was Solomonic indeed: Continue with the black/blue ink for original drafting but green/red ink may be used at later stages to indicate the modifications made; official hierarchy was duly indicated for the privilege of using green/red ink![13]

Arun Shourie also has some good advice for reforming the system: "Those in Government who want to change things should not chase individual cases — no one can solve the problems of the number of individuals who are bound to be buffeted by the workings of a ministry or department. Instead, he should devote the limited energy he has, and the even more limited time he is going to have at the post, to altering the system".[14]

A recent World Bank and International Finance Corporation (IFC) report bemoans the fact that India and other developing countries are tying up their formal economies in red tape. Indian entrepreneurs face particularly difficult obstacles. The country's regulations are more cumbersome than elsewhere in South Asia (not a challenging benchmark) when it comes to setting up a business, labour regulations, simple court procedures, and bankruptcy. The contrast with China is even more striking. This is, in fact, the third time the World Bank and IFC have published a *Doing Business* report. The number of countries ranked has increased from 145 in 2004-05 to 155 in 2005-06. According to the study, the key constraints in doing business are not always the number of procedures but time and money spent on them. India's overall ranking is 116th out of 155 and is bettered not just by China but also by all of South Asia (with the exception of Afghanistan). Pakistan (at 60th rank) is rated as much more business friendly than India. Dealing with licenses in India requires 20 procedures and 270 days and — believe it or not — insolvency procedures take 10 years![15] No one really expected India to be at the top of the doing-business pecking order, as New Zealand is today, but that current ranking remains dismal is indeed a matter of grave concern. Given the pace at which other countries are reforming, India has to guard against finding itself at the bottom of the heap with Sudan, Chad, Burkina Faso, and Congo.

Tavleen Singh had this diagnosis regarding India's awful ranking: "India's problem is a bureaucracy that has made an art of making the dead hand of the government even more dead."[16]

Poor performance in economic matters by India's bureaucracy causes concern to all observers including international economic analysts, especially members of the Indian Diaspora. Thus, Prof. T.N. Srinivasan, Chairman of the Economics Department at Yale University has called India's "wooden" bureaucracy "a major threat to India's economic ambitions." The comment was made at a seminar on "India-China Relations" organized jointly by the Woodrow Wilson International Center for Scholars and the Asia Society in Washington, D.C. in late-November/early-December 2001.[17]

Prof. Devesh Kapoor states in a similar vein in the *Harvard Magazine:* "At the core of problems that plague India lies the Indian state itself. India's elite bureaucracy, once a bastion of probity, has become politicized." Kapoor also draws attention to another important shortcoming — weakness in civil society: "The problems stemming from an unaccountable polity and bureaucracy are, of course, compounded by a citizenry whose social divisions hamper collective action."[18]

How much improvement can be realistically expected from streamlining the procedures and cutting down on paper work can be seen from the results reported by a U.S. government office — the

National Security Agency's Travel Office: "Before the reforms, it took 79 days to process the paperwork for a business trip. Now the time for paperwork is down 93 per cent, and the office is ranked by *Business Travel News* in the top four of all American businesses, alongside Hewlett Packard, Banker Trust, and Texas Instruments...There is no defect in bureaucrats that keeps them from being effective." They are held back and their efforts frustrated by procedural obstacles, which come in the way.[19] The same source reported that during one year alone "Clinton Administration... eliminated over 16,000 pages of rules out of 130,000 and...(was) revising another 30,000, a prodigious start towards a government which allows room for judgment on the spot.

It may, however be added that reforming administrative procedures alone would not solve the problem of the growing corruption in civil services and in life in India in general as the problem has become deeply embedded in society and now seems to be far worse than the exaggerations of the most cynical. Talking of corruption in civil services, B.K. Nehru observed some years ago: "Today over half of the IAS have joined the politicians in corrupt practices. They may, if they wish, seek satisfaction in the fact that among the politicians the percentage on a conservative basis is well over 80 per cent. It is a matter of credit to the strength of the ICS tradition that they resisted the temptation for so long...The position of the Indian Police Service is even worse because they are not regarded as implementers and enforcers of the law, but members of the private army of the Chief Minister."[20]

A *polite* statement about corruption on the part of politicians and civil servants was made years ago by T.N. Seshan: "The IAS is a brothel and the politicians, its pimps!" Another former Cabinet Secretary, T.S.R. Subramaniam, also worries deeply about the problem: "What is of concern is that the proportion of such corrupt elements is sharply on the increase in recent times. Whereas at one time, we could point out the odd undesirable officer, the time may not be far off when we may be hard put to identify an honest, able officer."[21] A senior member of the IPS, Prakash Singh, had also said the same thing earlier based on his long experience in handling corruption and the broader issues of law enforcement: "In the early Sixties we used to talk about and count dishonest officers...Today, we count the number of honest officers, a tribe in danger of extinction."[22]

It seems that a number of fresh entrants to civil services eagerly look forward to making money illegally. A retired bureaucrat and now a member of the Second Administrative Reform Commission (SARC) refers to cases where newly recruited candidates joining administrative services submitted property returns to the tune of crores (a crore equals ten million) of rupees in anticipation of the windfall awaiting them![23]

In the international setting, we have the dubious distinction of being rated amongst the most corrupt nations. The Transparency International ranked India as a lowly 90 on its Corruption Perception Index for 2004 (score of 2.8 on a scale of zero to ten), falling in the company of countries like Gambia, Malawi, and Tanzania. Corruption costs the Indian taxpayer around U.S. $7 billion annually![24] The situation is so bad that only drastic reform of the civil service and, more importantly, elimination of corruption in the political system will, hopefully, solve the problem.

It may be added that numerous individual activists and NGOs are doing some valuable anti-corruption work. A forthcoming book by Prof. Rob Jenkins of the University of London, *The politics of Exposure: Democracy, Transparency and Anti-Corruption in India,* examines the question: How anti-corruption activism, by articulating its demands as rights-based claim, has created new democratic spaces.[25]

- Introducing transparency in operations, which would ensure accountability and check corruption at the same time. In general, decisions by officials are taken behind closed doors and secrecy characterizes government functioning. This needs to be changed: bureaucrats need to share more information with the public and introduce openness in decision-making. Achieving that would necessitate amendments to the Official Secrets Act (OSA) as well as the Civil Services Code of Conduct. S.S. Meenakshisundaram suggests that "the existing grievance redressal centres in all offices should be converted into public facilitation centres, with people encouraged to obtain information relevant to their needs."[26]
- Providing protection to whistleblowers who expose wrongdoing.
- Enforcing and expanding the Freedom of Information

legislation. The Right to Information (RTI) Act passed by the government in 2002 is extremely weak and, thus, is not achieving the desired results. The Commonwealth Human Rights Initiative called the draft rules under the Act "a pre-emptive move to undermine the efforts of the civil society to improve the law…The draft set of Rules…is so weak it has only five clauses." Among other deficiencies, the cost to obtain information is high. "In a country where over 60 per cent of the people live on less than Rupees 100 per day, it is insulting to ordain that the cost of one application will be Rs. 50, and that this must be paid by demand draft or bank cheque! Moreover, copies of documents will be charged at Rs. 5 per page."[27] (The usual copying charge at public photostat machines ranges only from 75 Paise to one Rupee per page, and even lower for bigger copying jobs.)

The tardy execution of the provisions of the RTI Act can be seen with reference to the experience of West Bengal where the state missed the October 12, 2005 deadline to implement the legislation. The office of the Chief Information Commissioner was slated to start functioning from March 1, 2006 but this deadline, too, was missed; the RTI Website remains incomplete.[28] The Official Secrets Act — basically unchanged since its 1923 enactment date — is one significant hindrance in getting information from the traditionally opaque system of governance in India. Veerappa Moily, Chairman of SARC finds OSA a 'convenient smokescreen' to deny the public access to government information.[29]

In early June 2006, the Second Administrative Reforms Commission submitted a detailed report on RTI — as the initial subject for its first interim report to the government, *Right to Information: Master Key to Good Governance.* The following are its major recommendations:

- The Official Secrets Act, 1923 (OSA) should be repealed, and suitable safeguards to protect security of State should be incorporated in the National Security Act. The OSA in its current form is incongruous with the regime of transparency in a democratic society.
- Complete reorganization of public records is a precondition for effective implementation of RTI. A Public Records Office

should be established in each State as a repository of expertise to monitor, supervise, and inspect all public records.

- Information Commissions set up in the States should be entrusted with the responsibility and authority to monitor the implementation of the RTI Act in all public offices. At least half the members of the Information Commissions should be drawn from non-Civil Service background.
- Clear and unambiguous guidelines need to be evolved to determine which NGOs would come under the purview of the RTI Act.
- States may be advised to establish independent public grievance redressal authorities, which should work in close cooperation with the Information Commission.
- Certain safeguards should be introduced to discourage frivolous and vexatious requests for information to ensure that the system is not overloaded and discipline and harmony are not jeopardized.
- A roadmap should be charted out for effective implementation of the RTI Act in the Legislature and Judiciary at all levels.

The Commission has made specific recommendations, and suggested measures to implement each of them. Detailed recommendations pertain to a variety of issues, including civil service conduct rules and office procedures, record keeping, capacity building and awareness generation, and the exercise of power to remove difficulties.

An excellent example of the power of access to information about official actions was reported in late 2004 from Indonesia. A law lecturer, Saldi Isra of West Sumatra province of Indonesia, had acquired three years earlier a copy of the provincial budget to find that legislators had raised their pay and perks *twelve-fold!* He started a campaign against this blatant loot and soon the movement spread to all parts of the country making Isra one of Indonesia's top graft busters. In May 2004, a court in West Sumatra convicted 43 legislators (out of a total of 55) on charges of misappropriation of funds and sentenced them to prison terms of up to 27 months each — a decision hailed extraordinary for the Indonesian judicial system.[30]

In India, public awareness and activism have — at times — acted as a check on corruption. Thus, the politically conscious public of

Kerala has managed to secure many transparent official dispensations and generally to make life miserable for corrupt employees.

In any case, involvement of citizens in governance at various levels ought to be a key ingredient of democratic functioning. NGOs and other private entities should be utilized wherever possible. As society becomes more complex, government agencies cannot succeed in delivering all services or executing all programs on their own; they can become more successful by creating collaborative efforts that reach across departments/agencies, across levels of government, and across the non-profit and private sectors.

In the United States, a recent study by the IBM Corporation found that of the six trends of a more successful government, "Engaging Citizens" and "Using (private) Networks and Partnerships" were two important ones.[31]

However, not much improvement in bureaucratic functioning or in eliminating corruption can take place in India without checking all undue political interference. Bureaucrats are routinely pressurized by politicians to bend rules and manipulate the system; while the situation has become extremely serious lately, the practice is by no means new. Dharma Vira had faced problems, like most civil servants do, in dealing with ministers and political appointees. Decades ago, he had serious difficulties in working with V.K. Krishna Menon as he recounts in his autobiography. Menon "expected the officers to anticipate his wishes and to put up proposals accordingly." Dharma Vira's views on the duties of a civil servant were different; he felt that "A civil servant is paid to advise according to his conscience, to take orders thereafter and then carry them out conscientiously. In this respect Krishna Menon thought that I was being difficult…I insisted that he could not expect me to give advice which I did not consider to be correct."[32]

In Pondicherry — as elsewhere in the states and union territories (U.T.s) of India — politicians love to pressurize officials to toe the line, to do the politicians' bidding. One minister, in particular, was a specialist in bullying officials to carry out his commands — even his unstated wishes. He was not averse to hectoring and humiliating the unfortunate soul(s) in an open meeting. The minister's proclivities had to be kept in check by the higher ups, not heeding the minister's stand that such "interference" by an appointed head of the administration amounted to thwarting the popular mandate of the electorate; many politicians, of course, feel that they are the *sole* protectors of the public interest and the nation's good, and are entitled to a *carte blanche!* Such vainglorious ideas and misconceptions, of course, form important under-currents affecting the political leaders' relationship with civil servants.

Political leaders at the state/U.T. level feel more empowered to pressurize their local cadres (provincial civil service and others, and lower-level officials) compared to their dealings with members of All-India Services who, fortunately, are entitled to constitutional protections. Such protections serve as excellent safeguards — worthy of continuation (with some modifications) — even though they provide a shield to many an inefficient and unresponsive civil servant of the All-India cadres.

Politicians are able to regularly misuse their power over the bureaucracy because they enjoy — among other things — the absolute, unencumbered right to transfer or even suspend officials. However, sadly, many officers willingly cooperate with the ministers on a *quid pro quo* basis — getting good postings and garnering other favours, especially protection against charges of inefficiency and corruption (the politician, in effect, acting as Godfather).[33]

In India, transfers have attracted a lot of attention over the years as the power to move a bureaucrat has been grossly and unashamedly used by political leaders, with some officers shunted from place to place well within a year and sometimes even within a few months! This is certainly true in Uttar Pradesh, the author's home state. There, a survey had shown that the tenure of a collector averaged eight months and that of the head of the district police, from four to six months! Surely, other states are not immune to this affliction. Even at the Centre, the average term of secretaries to the government turned out to be just eleven months, according to a quick survey conducted by N.C. Saxena when he was Secretary of the Planning Commission.[34]

It appears that postings and transfers constitute a major component of ministers' duties. T.S.R. Subramaniam mentions in this connection his conversation with the secretary of the revenue department: "When I asked him about his relationship with the minister, [the secretary] told me jokingly, 'we have a good division of work.' The minister deals with the important work of postings and transfers…and I deal with the rest of the work, including revenue policy."[35]

At times, officers are suspended on whims of the concerned minister. Fortunately, for members of All-India Services, there are some protections so all that the politicians can do to harass them is to order transfers to *hard* stations, and do it frequently. This right the politicians have misused with impunity, paying no attention to its adverse effects on administration, the feelings of the affected bureaucrats, or to the public outcry for that matter. Politicians will always want to retain the power of transferring civil servants as this produces a large income through an implicit lucrative system — the highest bidder getting the best posts; auctioning is one chosen method to maximize the profit from corruption since the politician may not know the economic rent (bribes, etc.) that a post commands. Hilton L. Root of the Hoover Institution in the United States has fully grasped the intricacies of the Indian transfer system. He states: "The system fosters innovation to improve the private yield on posts because ambitious bureaucrats must recoup their investment to acquire additional resources for subsequent auctions. There is little incentive to produce public output efficiently because job performance does not influence promotions; those are decided by seniority." This results in an unending cycle of inefficiency and corruption. For this reason, the politician would not like to reform the bureaucratic structure. Root adds: "A concentrated liquid market for the sale of posts throughout India exists in the centralized administrative service. Concentrating the bidders further maximizes the amount politicians can earn when they sell the posts to bidders who know the value of the positions."[36]

Why talk of administrative reforms when the government can't even correct this simple problem? Politicians are getting away with unfair transfers of civil servants who do not do the politicians' bidding and do not help them earn money illegally, or object to the doling out of favours based on political or other inappropriate considerations. Everybody just talks about the blight, a practice that is not only unjust but also affects productivity adversely. It seems the leaders *like to talk the talk but do not want to walk the walk!* How difficult would it be to issue an ordinance right away and then pass legislation to the effect that a bureaucrat will remain in one station, say, for three years? This is the usual practice in the Foreign Service. If a bureaucrat does not perform or commits a misdemeanor or even a big crime, punish the person there itself, *but do not transfer.* What sense does it make to transfer the problem with the bureaucrat to another station? All that the recommended solution needs is *the political will* — the leaders denying themselves an unjust and nefarious tool for getting at the civil servant. Under the enabling legislation, rules could be framed outlining a transfer policy that considers suitability of the officer for the proposed posting in view of his qualifications and experience; past postings; length of service; and a compassionate consideration of the officer's personal circumstances (e.g. school-age children, special medical needs, etc.).[37]

Of course, the new transfer regulations should lay down all necessary procedures. B.G. Deshmukh, a former Cabinet Secretary, suggests that transfers be managed by "a system of Service Boards comprising senior bureaucrats who — and who alone — order the transfers, unlike now when a Minister orders a transfer on the flimsiest of pretexts. And alongside this Service Board, there should be some system of redressal of grievances quickly because tribunals are time-consuming. I would suggest that, like in some European countries, we follow the system of an Ombudsman — an Ombudsman is more time-bound and effective and he should be instituted along with the Service Board." Deshmukh also states that bureaucracy should be *lean* and well paid. "The problem today is that there are too many government servants and if there are too many of them, they work to keep themselves in business."[38]

It is gratifying to note that Prime Minister Manmohan Singh had raised the issue of transfers with the Chief Ministers soon after coming to power. However, action is needed at the Central level also and the P.M. might as well initiate action there as a comprehensive package and guide the states for action at their levels.

In these days of unfair — and frequently perversion- and extortion-driven — transfer policies, and bureaucrats, on their part, vying for good postings (using connections, so-called *jacks,* and humoring and bribing the powers that be), the conduct of earlier civil servants (who normally learnt about their transfers from official gazette notifications) would seem unbelievable. Dharma Vira had once turned down a transfer because it had been made on the basis of a recommendation from his father (Raja Jwala Prasad)! The incident is narrated in some detail in his autobiography.[39] In sharp contrast to the character of the then young ICS officer, bureaucrats these days hanker after choice postings.[40]

Apropos of the deteriorating character of civil servants, P.K. Gupta, a senior bureaucrat, refers to the loss of backbone on the part of bureaucrats: "It was said in the context of the Emergency of 1975 that, when they were asked to bend, they chose to crawl. How is it now that they tend to crawl even before anybody asks them even to bend?" He evaluates the change over a 35-year period of his civil service, citing the example of an assistant who recorded an adverse note on a file that had suggested a foreign trip by a minister. This note was duly endorsed by the section officer who stated that "no public purpose was likely to be served by the foreign tour" (giving reasons for his adverse recommendation), and that mere invitation by a foreign country "could be no adequate justification for spending scarce foreign exchange on the tour." This recommendation was upheld and the minister must have angrily unpacked his bags! Gupta feels that now, with the metamorphosis and dilution of moral standards, "even very senior officers of the level of joint secretary and above would much rather prefer to curry favour with the powers that be by supporting the worst proposal."

Regarding the point as to who is more responsible for the rot in the country's governance — the politician or the bureaucrat, Gupta quotes an old timer, an ex-chief secretary, as saying without the slightest hesitation that "the bureaucrat was the biggest culprit." He had explained it thus: "After all, the politician has more compulsions as he depends entirely on elections which involve huge financial outlay and do not necessarily encourage selfless public service but the permanent civil servant has a secure job." However, "today's officer is not prepared to make the slightest sacrifice...he does not mind being dubbed a *chamcha* or a bootlicker…Today's successful officer sees to it that only 'acceptable' recommendations are put up after prior consultations and everybody is happy even if the larger public interests may suffer."[41]

The decline in standards of uprightness and dedication is also outlined by Timir Kuran in a term paper on Indian Bureaucracy. Based on his twelve years of service in the IAS (including a stint at the Lal Bahadur Shastri Academy in Mussorie where he had an opportunity to teach and evaluate new recruits in the Service) prior to his coming to the United States, Kuran feels the areas of decline are in terms of a grudging and reluctant acceptance of the 'inevitability' of giving in to the whims of politicians, procrastination (possibly as a solution to politicization), demanding high dowries at the time of marriage, diminishing work ethic, tendency to evade responsibility, and in many cases the 'creep' of the acceptance of the 'inevitability' of corruption. "The will to stand up and be counted, and to be firm, is no longer universally found."[42]

Many press people, of course, have written about the nexus between corrupt politicians and pliable bureaucrats. To quote an eminent journalist — Kuldip Nayar: "Indira Gandhi, then a babe in the woods of politics, was able to master the Congress party's split with the help of officers in her secretariat. They told her how to employ the police and income tax and excise directorates to win or break a politician. She and her son, Sanjay Gandhi, built on that understanding, some years later, an illegal structure of power, which played havoc during the Emergency. Bureaucrats...do not seem to mind how the rulers make use of them. There are few conscientious objectors left. How many orders, both oral and written, did they [bureaucrats] defy [during the emergency]? Did anyone of them come to the rescue of a critic who was harassed or detained without trial? Now the civil service has got into the habit of doing unsavory jobs, without even being told."[43]

Madhav Godbole feels that civil servants and their associations should do more to stand up for what is right and stop looking at disturbing developments "with equanimity and typical Hindu detachment...They seem to have no interest in maintaining professional integrity and the fair name and reputation of the service to which they belong. There is no desire for any self-introspection in order to improve the performance and the image of the service. There is no courage of conviction to stand up and resist blatant political interference or injustice done to its members."[44]

While the author agrees with the analysis by Gupta and Godbole — laying a noticeable part of responsibility for corruption on the bureaucrat, he is not sure whether that responsibility is greater than that of the politician. Isn't politician the *leader,* a representative of the masses, and the legislator, who has the duty to chart out the country's progress and lay down policies for achieving the goals of all-round development? He/she is more powerful, is in a *superior* position. While it will remain a moot point as to who is the *major* culprit — the bureaucrat or the politician — to the author the latter's responsibility seems to be greater.

Fortunately, there still are some officers — albeit a small number — who will not cave in; there have been a number of martyrs for the cause of propriety and principles — including P.S. Appu (who left the service on an issue of principle); P.R. Rajagopal (removed by Indira Gandhi from his post as Delhi's police chief because he refused to carry out an illegal order and later retired prematurely as DG-

CRP); and M.N. Buch (also took early retirement, eight years before the due date — again on a matter of principle which led to differences with the Chief Minister of Madhya Pradesh). They all did the honourable thing, accepting the parameters set — fairly or unfairly — by the system. As stated by Buch himself: "A civil servant, whilst in the system, has to function within its constraints. He must do his job honestly and efficiently and must certainly curb administrative malpractices to the best of his ability...If he finds himself unable to adjust to the system, he must leave it and pursue individual course outside the service."[45] However, before doing this, the bureaucrat should fight hard for justice for himself, for the system, and in general national interest.

The measures discussed here (by no means an exhaustive list) would go a long way towards achieving the important objective of having an efficient and honest administration. In this connection, the setting up of a Central Vigilance Commission is a development that can be helpful in cleansing the system. However, an effective *legal framework* would be needed to achieve the desired result. In the opinion of N. Vittal, Central Vigilance Commissioner, we really need a law "which will provide for confiscation of ill-gotten wealth without the type of delays and hesitations we have. If every person knows, be it a businessman, politician, or a bureaucrat, that if he gets ill-gotten wealth and it will be confiscated, then the burden of proof will be on him, to prove that he got it legitimately...I am increasingly realizing that till the time such a law is brought in, we will not be able to control the pervasive corruption."[46] Of course, as indicated earlier, much more will have to be done in addition to passing such legislation to stem the tide of corruption.

IX

END JOB RESERVATIONS

O, that clear honor was purchased by the merit of the wearer.
—Shakespeare

There has been a growing opposition to the reservation system in government employment because it disregards merit. Reservations were initially set to end after a fixed number of years but these have kept on going and going, and growing! The opposition to reservations is based, *inter alia,* on the following considerations:

- The quota system devalues merit and adversely affects the quality of governance. In the United States, quotas are shunned for this reason — *affirmative* action *yes*, quotas *no,* to preserve a *merit-based* system; affirmative action means help to disadvantaged groups (who, mainly Black Americans, had been blatantly discriminated against and held back in the past) in the field of education through scholarships, etc., placement in good schools (including Ivy League institutions like Harvard, Princeton, and Yale, for very talented students), targeted recruitment, and so on. But, quotas are not liked, and have actually been declared illegal by courts. Unlike India, the U.S. aims at making people equal at *the starting line*, <u>not</u> at *the finishing line.* Merit is sacrificed further in India when even promotions are granted on the basis of reservations.
- The benefit of reservations was originally granted for a fixed period and it should now come to an end. In any case, there is no justification at all for extending it to the second, third, and subsequent generations of the *same* family! Why should, for example, the son/daughter of a reserved category minister, chief minister, a university vice-chancellor, secretary to the government of India or another senior bureaucrat, successful

professional, or a very well-off businessman, be entitled to the advantage of reservations in selection and also in promotion? With the same families availing of reservations from generation to generation, some backward communities by now have a relatively large cluster of their members in civil services. This trend is accentuated by better performance of their candidates in competitive examinations due to the improved circumstances of their families.[1] Thus the process of correcting old inequities (most of which were real but some were inconsequential) has gone well beyond what was originally intended or what could be termed fair in the light of changed circumstances. This has created new inequities, *inter-group* (all), and particularly *intra-group* (within reserved categories themselves — between the so-called 'creamy layer' and other segments).[2]

- There are many *very* poor people among socially *forward* communities, too, who deserve help. So, why not consider *economic backwardness* as an important criterion for reservations?
- Discrimination against people belonging to reserved categories had been outlawed a long time ago and — with their entry in significant numbers in services, business, professions, etc., and the changed legal and social environment — the disadvantages have, for all practical purposes, disappeared. Taking a macro view, a substantial number of people from *all* groups are still in the grip of debilitating poverty and overall backwardness (despite sectors and regions of prosperity comparable to developed countries).[3]
- The improvement in the life of reserved categories over time was rightly foreseen by the leaders who wanted reservations to end at the end of the set period.

It would be a mistake to extend reservations to the private sector[4] for which some people are clamoring, and to expand it for admissions in educational institutions. However, heedless of the expected, substantial damage to meritocracy, the government announced in May 2006 extension of reservations in admissions of OBC candidates to professional institutions (27 per cent of total seats) — a retrograde step compounding earlier reservation follies. The resulting, disruptive protests, hunger strikes, and violence were indicative of a misguided policy afoot and its non-acceptance by a very large number of Indian citizens.

It should be noted in this context that a majority of the National Knowledge Commission (NKC) members has opposed the extension of reservations in central educational institutions as proposed by Union Human Resources Development Minister Arjun Singh. Six members, including Chairman Sam Pitroda, want *status quo* with regard to reservations; two members — Vice-Chairman Dr. P.M. Bhrgava and economist Dr. Jayati Ghosh — support the recommendation. However, even Bhargava wants the reservations subject to certain conditions; he wants reservations to be accompanied by expansion in educational facilities so that merit intakes are not reduced. Pitroda, speaking for the majority, stated that the issues — including compatibility with the goals of a knowledge society —"require more social debate and careful thought." Dr. Deepak Nayyar added: "After 50 years of reservation strategy, it is time for an alternative."[5] A little later, two members of the Knowledge Commission — Pratap Bhanu Mehta and Andre Beteille — took their opposition to a higher level by resigning from their membership! In separate, strongly worded letters to the P.M., they reiterated their commitment to the principle of social inclusion but questioned motives behind the quotas calling them detrimental to the development of a knowledge society. According to Mehta, the quota decision and the 'palliative' measures to defuse the resulting agitation violate 'four cardinal principles' that institutions in a knowledge-based society will have to follow. "They are not based on assessment of effectiveness, they are incompatible with the freedom and diversity of institutions, they more thoroughly politicize the education process, and they inject an insidious poison that will harm the nation's long-term interest." Beteille felt that: "We can either move forward and create centres of excellence or go along with demands of identity politics based on caste and community, but we cannot do both." He also referred to the deliberate 'cynical misrepresentation' of the recent amendment to the Constitution. "They are enabling provisions and not mandatory ones (for extending caste quotas) as they are being made out to be."[6]

The Prime Minister and his senior colleagues tried to have their way and *manage* the situation through suggestions like increasing seats in the IITs and medical colleges; effecting reservations gradually; involving the private sector in funding backward caste students; and so on. But these measures do not address the fundamental issue raised by the Knowledge Commission members and others: Reservations dealing body blows to the principle of *merit,* which would result — as in the past — in promoting *mediocrity.* However, going ahead with its plans, the government appointed on May 29, 2006 a 13-member Oversight Committee headed by Veerappa Moily, Chairman of the Second Administrative Reforms Commission, to monitor the implementation of reservation for OBCs in higher educational institutions. Also, three separate groups were established to draw up the modalities for implementing the decision in engineering and management institutions besides Central Universities.[7]

The Pan-IIT Alumni Association also wrote to the President of India and the Prime Minister to stop proposed reservation quotas for OBCs. The organization, which collectively represents approximately 150,000 alumni of the seven IITs, argued that, while it was supportive of affirmative action and creating equal opportunity for all, it did not believe a system of reservations was the correct approach. "We believe that meritocracy and excellence should be the guiding principles in implementing reforms," the body said. "Reservations and quotas along the lines of caste, creed, ethnicity, etc. have only served to divide people and are regressive and counterproductive to the fundamental goals of social change...IITs were setup for creating a group of Indians to be globally competitive. They were never created for mass education. Affirmative action should be applied for mass education at primary level, and not for institutions of excellence…IIT brand recognition has been hard won, and has played a very important role in the rising international esteem for India and Indians in recent years."[8]

The subject of reservations should be looked at in the context of the country's long-term interests. One should not forget that meritorious performance by Indian companies attracts foreign business. Only by being highly competitive in the global arena can India attract large investments and collaborative ventures; the same applies for India's ventures abroad and exports of trained manpower. A foreign company will set up a BPO in Gurgaon, Bangalore, Hyderabad, or Chennai based on competitive cost-benefit advantage flowing from an efficient operation, *not* on the basis of compassion for India's disadvantaged population or for furthering U.S. India friendship! Similarly, only by providing world-class medical services can India attract more medical tourism — a relatively new but growing business for Indian hospitals. In matters of life and death (literally), only meritorious performance by healthcare professionals would count. The country has to realize that in an increasingly knowledge-based society, merit will remain the key determinant of progress.

Quite unsurprisingly, the government's determination to introduce merit-devaluing additional quotas led to the enactment of Central Educational Institutions (Reservation in Admissions) Bill, 2006, for 27 per cent reservations for OBCs in Central-Government-funded educational institutions including the IITs and IIMs; the reservations will be introduced in phases over three years. However, the government's plans have met an impediment: The Supreme Court (SC) has ordered to put on hold the execution of the Act. The government was reportedly contemplating to move the SC with a request to vacate the order, and to refer it to a Constitution Bench.

Unfortunately, the reservations express (train) may not be stopping (except for re-fueling) as there are further destinations to reach! Just recently, a study on the status of India's Muslim population came out — the Sachar Commission Report — which could be mined for justification for jobs/admissions quotas for that community. The report contains very useful and interesting statistics — for instance, the fact that only 4 per cent Muslims graduate from schools (against their population of some 14 per cent of the total) and that, despite the faith's tenet of full equality and 'brotherhood', their exist some caste hierarchies in the Muslim community. *Ajlafs* and *Arjals* reportedly correspond to the Hindu OBCs and Scheduled Castes, respectively.[9] Although the Commission makes no recommendations for reservations for the Muslim community, *per se,* many people in the country are worried that political leaders may use backwardness of Muslims on a number of criteria to play 'vote-bank' politics and set quotas for the community. Some politicians may be tempted to derive benefit through such reservations (or promises/indications of future action in this regard) in Assembly elections in Uttar Pradesh (U.P.), set for early 2007. U.P. happens to be the largest state in terms of population and it also has a relatively high proportion of Muslims. This is actually the state where the Congress party's decline started in the late-1980s when Muslims and OBCs abandoned it. Hence there is concern in some circles about the 'vote-bank' politics coming into play. Thus, according to Saisuresh Sivaswamy, quotas for Muslims may not be "a simple matter...to strengthen minorities, they harbour a deeper game-plan for the revival of Congress."[10]

However, while the motivation for reservations will remain a moot point, the nature of motivation does not really alter the fact that quotas are inimical to the principles of meritocracy and that there are other, effective and equitable, ways to achieve desired social goals.

Numerous observers have commented on the Sachar Commission report; some have sharply questioned the methodology of inquiry adopted and the coverage/contents of the report, pointing out that the panel did not do enough to go into the causes behind the current status of the community.[11]

Ashok Desai states in this connection: "The government is likely to infer [from the Commission's report] that Muslims are discriminated against in regular jobs, and to be tempted to reserve jobs for them…That would be a mistake based on misdiagnosis. The basic disadvantages of Muslims are specialization in declining industries, poor education, and fluency in a language with no economic value. In my view, the government should put the money…into the modernization of the industries Muslims are specialized in — fabrics, leather, tobacco, auto repair and electricals."[12] M.J. Akbar also expresses similar views about the causative factors and remedial action: "Economic empowerment through credit to entrepreneurs is definitely more effective than a squabble over clerical jobs…the key to the future [for Muslims] lies in education, and more specifically, English education. Urdu is a beautiful language, but it is not a language in which jobs can be found anymore."[13]

In response to a question on Sachar Commission's Report leading to likely quotas for Muslims, N.R. Narayanamurthy (Infosys Chief) stated his opposition to reservations in employment and in educational institutions and suggested, instead, "providing better attention and training…as the best way to bring people up."[14]

It is hoped that the Sachar Commission Report will not lead to the creation of additional reservations and worsen the existing, troublesome divisions within the country — going from *caste* divide (augmented by caste quotas) to *religious* divide. That there is a clear need to take meaningful and urgent action to counter the deprivation of Muslims, wherever existing, is incontrovertible. But this should be done through affirmative measures rather than by sowing seeds of further communal divide in the country for shortsighted political or other considerations. The Commission itself refers to the need for focus on 'inclusive development' and 'mainstreaming' of the Muslim community while 'respecting diversity.'

Although their practice has not been duly emphasized — apparently because of narrow political considerations — affirmative action and the value of merit-based selection have been talked about in India for a long time. For example, Hardwari Lal — who was well-credentialed to speak on the topic as a former member of the Punjab Public Service Commission, vice-chancellor (of two universities), jurist, and political leader/parliament member — had this to say well over a decade ago: "Apolitical civil services, recruited by a civil service commission, solely on the basis of merit, are among the chief attributes of the parliamentary form of government of the Westminster model. The USA, for long afflicted by the vice of spoils system in the matter of civil services, has will-nilly veered round to the British view that…the state is best served by persons inducted in the administration on the basis of merit, to the exclusion of all other considerations. The firm tradition of an objective, powerful and efficient bureaucracy has well served France, which has witnessed since 1815 five changes in the form of government. The great irony of the Indian situation is that the governments, particularly at the state level, have given the go-by to merit." After describing some scandalous departures from merit-based selections in Punjab and Haryana, Hardwari Lal gave his reaction: Dr. Rajendra Prasad (President of the Constituent Assembly of Independent India and the country's first President), who counted the creation of 'independent' Public Service Commissions for the Union and the states "among the invaluable gifts of founding fathers to the people of India," would have felt extremely miserable.[15]

On the subject of reservations, Hardwari Lal felt that "the very idea of reservation implies that some less meritorious persons should be acceptable for services of the state or the Union. Now, when the Constitution was framed, care was taken to maintain a balance between efficiency of administration and social justice. But with the intrusion of populism in Indian politics, this balance has been rudely shaken. The states of Tamil Nadu and Karnataka where this has happened may be readily mentioned…But the situation in such matters is indivisible. It may well be that other states will emulate these two, to win 'vote-banks'. Haryana is already moving in that direction, though somewhat cautiously. The Cabinet recently decided to include a number of peasant communities in the 'reservation fortress'. It may soon want to exceed the limit of 50 per cent reservation of civil posts under the government and of seats in educational institutions. *It is unfortunate that "remedial education" for backward sections of society has not occurred to the powers that be as an ideal substitute of reservations, as a means to bring these sections in the mainstream."* (Emphasis added.)[16, 17]

To conclude, the right policy would be to do away with *all* reservations — based on caste/tribe/religion/creed/sect/region or other divisive considerations — and to follow *affirmative* principles wherever warranted, in jobs or in educational institutions. Models of corrective action for all disadvantaged sections (backward or forward) followed in other countries (including the United States[18]) should be studied for formulating plans suiting the conditions prevailing in India.

X

GOVERNMENT'S PROPOSED REFORMS

Let's see if the bureaucrats allow it to happen.

— *J.R.D. Tata*

(His reaction when informed in 1991, towards the end of his life, that the government had started thinking about bureaucratic reforms.)[1]

The new government, ever since it came to power, has been making noises about reforming the hydra-headed bureaucracy.[2] Prime Minister Manmohan Singh, in his very first Independence Day speech in August 2004 (soon after the new government had taken over), said that the time had come for evolving a code of best practices at all levels of government; the reforms should cover all political parties, the bureaucracy, and the functioning of legislatures and the electoral process.

One major proposal advanced by the Prime Minister relates to early selection of potential civil servants, i.e., *catch 'em young!* Under the proposed scheme, an all-India entrance examination will be held for Class XII students on the pattern followed for recruitment to defense services, law colleges, and the IITs; selected students would join a National Academy for a five-year course. At the end of three years, those passing the examinations satisfactorily will be awarded an undergraduate degree. The best among them will be absorbed in the civil service on the basis of merit and choice while the rest can go out and seek other opportunities — further studies or jobs. The reservation quotas will be continued.

Selected candidates at that stage who have been given their service allotments can then go in for a two-year service-specific course. The candidates who do not perform well during the two-year course could go out into the market with an MBA-equivalent degree.

The proposal appears good for Services where generalists are needed (IAS, etc.) but not where specialized training is required —

in fields like medicine, engineering, and agriculture. Obviously, one new academy (or more?) could not be expected to cover all specializations; anyway, for these disciplines good institutions already exist — the IITs, regional engineering colleges, medical colleges, State Agricultural Universities (SAUs — one or more in most states), and other technical/specialized institutions. A high proportion of these are world-class institutions, especially, the IITs, whose graduates are in great demand in the United states and other developed countries. The training imparted in these good places cannot easily, and need not, be duplicated; in any case, the cost of such a move would be very high. A sensible solution would be to utilize the graduates of the proposed new academy (ies) only for the generalist jobs. Other civil services should be manned by technically qualified people.

Earlier a recommendation was made about a civil service with various components: *Management-centric S*ervices (like the IAS) and *development-centric* Services like medical and public health, engineering and agricultural, etc. The graduates of the proposed academy(ies) would be suitable for the former group (management-centric Services).The framers of training programs should keep these and other training and recruitment-related proposals in mind while developing the structure of any new institute(s).

In this context, comments will not be out of place about the present training facilities for civil service probationers at the Lal Bahadur Shastri Academy of Administration in Mussorie. Experienced civil servants-turned-teachers and faculty recruited from outside do a good job of teaching and guiding, and also conducting research in selected fields in accordance with their present training mandate.[3]

That the training at the Mussorie Academy is good can also be appreciated in the light of the fact that graduating probationers perform satisfactorily, including, for example, those who got in on the basis of mandated quotas and may not have possessed the starting academic proficiency of candidates from the general (non-reserved) category. There are large reserved quotas in India for scheduled castes and scheduled tribes (SCs/STs), and for other backward castes (OBCs). For candidates from these categories, the scores in competitive examinations are usually lower — sometimes substantially — as they compete only among themselves for a large number of seats. But when the probationers come out, their overall performance is satisfactory not only for the open category (non-reserved) probationers but also for those from reserved categories — *for the type of work currently being done by civil servants, and because of not very challenging performance standards set for them, especially, in respect of developmental and welfare activities.*

One reform measure that has already been put into effect at the initiative of the Prime Minister relates to the deputation of members of the IAS and other Services to posts outside the country. A circular reportedly went out in August 2004, asking senior government officials to refrain from accepting short-term stints abroad. Even without knowing the details of this reform measure one would be inclined to agree with the rationale behind the P.M.'s move; the number of deputations have indeed become very large. The author met many such deputationists during the course of his foreign travels — personal or on official business — and while posted abroad. They were working as generalists as well as in all kinds of specialized fields like population planning, health issues, and social services. The World Bank and IMF in Washington, D.C. have a noticeable presence of Indian civil servants — seconded officially or holding regular jobs after resigning from government service.

People who are highly qualified, having specialized training in important fields in demand, complain that they seldom get deputation opportunities in their areas of expertise if they do not belong to All-India Services, especially the IAS, or to other cadres/offices of the government. Since senior bureaucrats take decisions regarding such deputations (as the requests usually come to them, especially from international, inter-governmental organizations), they tend to favour people from civil services. No wonder technical people/specialists feel left out. To illustrate, one professor at Haryana Agricultural University, who had worked as head of the Department of Agricultural Economics and also as dean of the College of Agriculture, was highly qualified to serve with the U.N. Food and Agriculture Organization (FAO), but the university usually was not informed about FAO vacancies which were notified to the Ministry of Food and Agriculture at Delhi. The concerned professor held a Ph.D. from an American university; was fully qualified academically, having had considerable experience of research, extension, and teaching; had published extensively; and had been the president of not only the top professional association of his discipline in India but also of the international association! But such individuals are seldom considered for any deputation to the FAO by the Ministry, which is busy placing people from its own ranks. An overwhelming number of deputation opportunities to U.N. agencies seem to go to government employees, especially those working at Delhi.[4]

Incidentally, the same is true of foreign training that is easily made available to IAS officers; a preponderant number, most probably all, are routinely sent abroad at government expense. Pankaj Vohra refers to a joke about our civil servants: "After the Central Secretariat, the maximum number of bureaucrats were in the universities of the United States!"[5] I know a large number of IAS officers who were sent abroad for training, including some who worked with me.[6] Ex-Cabinet Secretary T.N. Seshan, the author's colleague in the Planning Commission, had studied at Harvard. Usually such students did well and it was good they had been provided the opportunity. But shouldn't others in the government (and outside the government), especially the technocrats and specialists for whom advanced training in certain fields is not available in India, also be afforded more chances (than available at present) to study abroad? Both the cost-benefit ratio of the investment and *equity considerations* would justify spreading the government benefit around.

The P.M. has also made some recommendations about improving accountability — e.g. a serious appraisal of overall performance of bureaucrats after a set period of some years, and then decide about their future promotion track and other service prospects in order to chart out the entire career of a civil servant.

The government has been looking at past reports on reforms to see the applicability of their recommendations. Suggestions of outsiders would also be considered; the Prime Minister's Office (PMO) had requests pending from organizations/institutions like the India International Centre (IIC) at Delhi to organize academic debates among a wide section of society, including retired bureaucrats.

Two studies under examination by the government were: Report of the panel chaired by former Union Public Service Commission (UPSC) Chairman Surendra Nath (has inputs in areas such as placement and performance appraisal of civil servants), and by another group headed by P.C. Hota, also a former UPSC Chairman, that was to be looked at by a committee steered by Cabinet Secretary B.K. Chaturvedi. The Hota Committee had made some good proposals, e.g., lowering the eligibility age for entry into the civil service; new rules to allow attachment of ill-gotten property, acquired through *benami* (hidden identity) or *beimani* (dishonest) deals; a performance review every 15 years to ease out dishonest and inefficient officers; and amendment to the Constitution to enable dismissal of the corrupt.

These are good suggestions, by and large, but India's bureaucracy needs more reforms, of a rather radical nature. Tinkering with the system *as is* will not help much. It would be like the characterization by Toplady: "Mere outward reformation differs as much from regeneration as white-washing an old rotten house differs from pulling it down and building a new one in its place."[7] There is need to look at the basic civil service structure and the overall personnel needs of a growing and increasingly sophisticated economy of the 21st century, and to be willing to take new, non-trodden paths. In other words, one has to *start looking outside the box.* Thus, the government should consider: hiring part of the bureaucracy on short-term contracts (renewable when necessary or desirable) and contracting out some services to the private sector on economy and efficiency grounds. Such additional measures would complement the proposals made earlier, namely: setting up certain technical/specialized services to meet the demands of development; having outside entrants with outstanding credentials at the middle and senior ranks of the civil service; encouraging interchange of personnel among civil services, academia, and industry; changing the attitude of bureaucracy — making civil servants *civil* to the public (which, after all, makes it possible, through their taxes, to let them be pampered and feel all-important); and ending reservations, which devalue merit and have, in any case, already had an unduly long run.

Of course, the suggestions given here and in earlier sections do not add up to an exhaustive list; other measures have to be looked at and some new ones will certainly come to the fore when the whole matter of bureaucratic reforms is pursued earnestly, and not merely as an exercise in window-dressing.

In this context, an important, far-reaching set of administrative reforms for India's police forces was announced recently. However, it was not done by the executive branch of the government, nor ordained by the legislative branch, but ordered by the judicial branch — the Supreme Court (SC) of India! The apex court acted since the administration had been neglecting its duty to effect police reforms, particularly the comprehensive set of very good recommendations made by the National Police Commission (NPC) well over two decades ago. This is not the first instance of the SC performing an activist role — an unconventional thrust in the executive realm; earlier, the court had, for example, ordered substantive, specific action towards the cleanup of Delhi's environment.

The S.C.'s momentous judgment, passed on September 22, 2006, could greatly transform the way police forces in India are organized, operate, and controlled. The order vindicates the stand taken by a group of enlightened police officers led by Prakash Singh, former Director General of the Border Security Force (BSF), who had filed a public interest litigation (PIL) around ten years ago. They had sought a direction from the Court to the Union of India to frame a new Police Act on the lines of the Model Act drafted by the NPC in order to ensure that police is made accountable essentially and primarily to the law of the land and to the people.[8]

The NPC, constituted in 1977 by the Janata Party government, was a reaction to the abuse of the police system by Indira Gandhi-led Congress government to serve partisan interests, especially during the Emergency declared in 1975. A former highly regarded civil servant, Dharma Vira, was named the chairman of the Commission. It issued eight comprehensive reports between 1979 and 1981 — all masterpieces. However, the new government formed after Indira Gandhi's re-election looked upon these reports with disdain and action on their recommendations was frozen. But it will not be fair to indict the Congress party alone for the appalling indifference to the NPC recommendations. The other political parties, which were in power subsequently, did not exactly distinguish themselves in the matter of effecting reforms to make the police more professional, honest, and people-friendly.

It was under these circumstances — characterized by inaction and pronounced lack of political will to reform the police on the lines suggested by the NPC — that Prakash Singh and others had approached the apex court. Since then three committees had been formed to examine the subject. Action has been taken by the Home Ministry in a number of areas covered in the various reports, but it has been inadequate to address major problems because of the absence of political backing. And, unfortunately, the shortfall in action has been more in areas where reforms were badly needed.

The Home Ministry has also been hamstrung by the relative lack of enthusiasm on the part of state governments. The greatest cause of the apathy, however, is the apparent assessment by all political parties that they do not have much to gain from sweeping reforms that would free the police from political control and caprice. There is a perceived stake in perpetuating corruption and keeping the police as submissive as possible to the ruling political party.

It was this tardy and inadequate progress in carrying out the recommendations of the NPC that persuaded the Supreme Court to issue a history-setting judgment. The order displays an amazing understanding of the situation on the part of the court and as to what it would take to carry out meaningful reforms of the country's police system. In view of its path-breaking, activist judgment and far-reaching nature of the mandated reforms, salient features of the S.C. order are given below:

- *State Security Commission*: The state governments are directed to constitute such a body in every state to ensure that the state government does not exercise unwarranted influence or pressure on the state police, and for laying down the broad policy guidelines so that the state police always acts according to the laws of the land and the Constitution of the country.
- *Tenure of the DGP*: The Director General of Police of the state shall be selected by the state government from amongst the three senior-most officers of the Department who have been empanelled for promotion to that rank by the Union Public Service Commission on the basis of their length of service, very good record, and range of experience for heading the police force. Once he has been selected for the job, he should have a minimum tenure of at least two years irrespective of his date of superannuation.
- *Minimum Tenure of I.G. of Police and other officers*: Police officers on operational duties in the field (including the Station House Officer in-charge of a police station) shall also have a prescribed minimum tenure of two years.
- *Police Establishment Board*: There shall be such a Board in each state, which shall decide all transfers, postings, promotions, and other service-related matters of officers. It shall be a departmental body comprising the DGP and four other senior officers of the department. The Board shall also function as a forum of appeals for disposing of representations from police officers, and generally for reviewing the functioning of police in the state.
- *Police Complaints Authority*: There shall be such an Authority (PCA) at the district level to look into complaints against police officers, and another such Authority at the state

level. The district-level body may be headed by a retired District Judge while the one at the state-level, by a retired judge of the High/Supreme Court.

- *Separation of Investigation*: The investigating police shall be separate from the law and order police to insure speedier investigation, better expertise, and improved rapport with the people. It must, however, be insured that there is full coordination between the two wings.
- *National Security Commission*: The Central government shall also set up a National Security Commission to prepare a panel for being placed before the appropriate Appointing Authority, for selection and placement of Chiefs of the Central Police Organizations (CPOs), who should also be given a minimum tenure of two years. The Commission would also review from time-to-time measures to upgrade the effectiveness of these forces, improve service conditions of their personnel, ensure that there is proper coordination between them, and that the forces are generally utilized for the purpose they were raised and make recommendations in that behalf.

The Supreme Court has indeed rendered signal service to the country by giving the above landmark directions; end-December 2006 was set as the deadline for putting reforms in place. Although the S.C. judgment deals specifically with police reforms, the highlights of the order have been included here because the mandated measures have considerable, direct relevance to overall bureaucratic reforms.

Obviously, the subject of administrative reforms has to be handled at the level of *general reform measures* that apply to all civil services, and *specific reform measures* that deal with individual Services/ branches/activities of the government. In the context of the former (overall administrative reforms), the government — seemingly alive to gross shortcomings of governance and realizing that piecemeal measures under consideration would not be able to address fundamental structural and procedural problems of an outdated and outmoded system — has taken a significant, timely step: Appointment of the Second Administrative Reforms Commission (SARC). The Cabinet gave a nod to its establishment on April 8, 2005. A formal notification of the reforms panel's constitution was issued on August 31, 2005, charging it with the task of preparing a detailed blueprint to revamp the public administration system. The Commission comprises: Veerappa Moily, Chairman, and four Members — V. Ramachandran, Chairman, Centre for Management Development, A.P. Mukherjee, former Director, Central Bureau of Investigations (CBI), A.H. Kalro, Director, AES, Post-graduate Institute of Management, Ahmedabad; and Jayaprakash Narayan, National Coordinator, Lok Satta. Vineeta Rai, a senior IAS officer, was named Member-Secretary. The SARC, with status as a Commission of Inquiry, has come some 40 years after the first such body, headed by Morarji Desai, was set up in 1966 to make recommendations for reform and reorganization of the public administration system. The new panel was asked to submit its report within a period of one year.[9] However, its tenure was extended in mid-July, 2006 by one year, through August 31, 2007.

It was planned at the outset that the members of the Commission will have to be non-political. Official sources had said at the time: "We are deliberately appointing non-political members *so that bureaucrats accept whatever recommendations are made by the Commission.*" (Emphasis added)[10] If acceptance of the recommendations by the bureaucracy seems such an important consideration as to determine even the panel's membership, how could one expect far-reaching changes in the structure and in powers and privileges that civil servants have been enjoying for a very long time? After all, they are supposed to bless the recommendations if the above quote has any credence! This limitation does pose a worrisome prospect.

A 13-point terms of reference[11] wants the Commission to strengthen the framework for efficient, economical, sensitive, clean, objective, and agile administrative machinery. It will go into the issue of reorganization of ministries and departments and their role in the context of globalization. It will also define ethics in governance and suggest measures to strengthen pro-active vigilance, eliminate corruption and harassment of honest civil servants including limitation on executive discretion, and address systemic reluctance to punish the corrupt. The Commission will identify procedures, rules and regulations, and factors which lead to corruption; suggest measures to combat the evil along with arbitrary decision making; and propose a framework for their periodical review in consultation with stake-holders.

On relationship between political leaders and the permanent civil service, it will suggest improvements for a harmonious relationship and formulate a code of conduct for different organs of the government including these two. On issues of federal polity, the Commission will review operation of the federal relationship to improve the civil service performance that will include framework for continuing interaction between the centre and the states and harmonize different conditions of service prevalent across different states for All-India Services.

In the field of crisis management, the reforms panel will suggest ways to quicken the emergency response situation and ways to increase effectiveness and enhance preparedness. It will also suggest a framework to strengthen machinery to maintain public order conducive to social harmony and economic development. Capacity building for conflict resolution, too, will be looked into.

In an attempt to refurbish personnel administration, the Commission will review policy relating to all methods of recruitment, training, and placement and recommend changes. It will provide guidelines for enhancing performance of civil servants, improving methods of cadre management, focusing on career management and motivation, and linking performance to social and economic objectives and outcomes.

The other points in the terms of reference include capacity building in financial management systems at all levels of governance to ensure smooth flow of funds for programmes and projects, strengthening of internal audit systems, and institutionalizing a method of external audit, and assessment of their delivery. The Commission will also suggest steps to ensure effective administration at state and district levels by promoting and encouraging appropriate changes in administration.

The delivery mechanism of public utilities and civil services in local self-government and *panchayati raj* institutions will also be addressed. On citizen-centric administration, the Commission will seek to ensure accountability and transparent government by addressing issues of delegation, accountability and openness, and reduction in delays in delivery of services. On freedom of information, it will review the confidentiality classification of government documents, especially with reference to the Official Secrets Act and encourage transparency and access to non-classified data.

Veerappa Moily, Chairman of SARC, has been saying that the panel plans to stress technology and E-governance as the 'order of the day' and work out a delivery system that would adequately meet the needs of the populace. Thus, in his interview with the Indo-Asian

News Service (IANS) on September 8, 2005 — ahead of the Commission's first meeting — Moily had stated: "If the private sector could grow so rapidly with the aid of technology, why not the entire administrative machinery?" He assured that the thrust of the recommendations would be on a universal system driven by technology and pragmatism.

The Commission will also study administrative systems in other countries like Singapore, Sweden, Australia, and New Zealand so as to assimilate their best practices. But Moily warned: "Though some of the systems are good, a pluralistic country like India with a multitude of problems should have an indigenous system that does not ignore the social dimension. Towards that end we shall involve civil society, political parties and public institutions in our discussions to evolve a citizen-centric administration." The chairman believes that downsizing or rightsizing is not the real issue. "We have to go beyond that because there is no ready-made solution. There is no point in having a new structure without adequate legislative and legal protection. Instead of tinkering the present system, we will go for a major surgery of the entire system with sweeping reforms, so that an enabling environment is created for a transparent and efficient delivery of government services." Moily added: "The present system and procedures are outdated and ill- equipped to serve the people in the face of rapid changes taking place across the country on the socio-economic fronts…If India had to become a fully developed country by 2020, its system of governance would need a work culture with attitudinal changes to meet the growing aspirations of its billion-strong people."[12]

It is hoped that SARC will concentrate not only on making recommendations about effecting systemic and structural changes but will also devote due attention to changing the mindset of India's bureaucracy — from *administrative* to *managerial;* this would ensure performance and efficiency, civility, and promptness in delivery of government services. N.R. Narayanamurthy, Chairman of Infosys Technologies (one of the most successful IT companies in the world) puts very well the distinction between administration and management: "Administration is about conforming to and maintaining the *status quo;* it is about hierarchy based on titles and age. Management, unlike administration, is about a hierarchy based on value-addition and performance; it is about fostering innovation and excellence; it is about new ways of doing things…Administration is about sticking to the past while management is about adapting to dynamic change. Hence, administration is about operating as a system without feedback, while improvement based on feedback is at the core of management."[13]

Emphasis on *management* would certainly result in better planning and better execution. Indian bureaucrats — although known for being well endowed with intelligence — often fail as managers. According to Gurcharan Das, "Indians tend to blame ideology or democracy for their failures, but the problem is that they value *ideas* over *accomplishment*."[14] He cites the case of Delhi Metro as an example of successful execution: "Great strides are being made on the Delhi Metro not because the project was brilliantly conceived but because its leader sets clear, measurable goals, monitors day-to-day progress, and persistently removes obstacles. Most Indian politicians and civil servants, in contrast, fail to plan their projects well, monitor them, or follow through on them: their performance failures mostly have to do with poor execution."[15]

Such changes in attitudes and in approaches to achieving results on the ground would require a lot of prodding and pushing as Indian administrators, by and large, believe in *status quo;* they want to maintain the *quo* even when it has lost *status!* Normally, they do not want to navigate untrodden paths.[16]

Coming back to the administrative reforms panel, it appears that the Commission's terms of reference are wide enough to include all relevant issues directly or indirectly. Thus, now it all depends upon the diligence of the Members and the thoroughness with which they, and their staff, tackle the extremely important and urgent issues of proper governance. The country, and especially the more directly affected parties — while wishing the Commission well in discharging its onerous duties — await its findings and recommendations.

Realizing the value of getting its findings and recommendations to the government expeditiously, SARC had decided some time ago to submit reports in phases. Thus, it presented the first one, on right to information, to the Prime Minister on June 9, 2006. Other reports to come will cover subjects like crisis management, public order, and National Rural Employment Guarantee Scheme. And, in the second phase, the Commission proposes to submit reports on organizational structure of the central government, ethics in governance, refurbishing of administration, and local self-government and *panchayati raj* institutions.

XI

SUMMARY AND CONCLUSIONS

> *The significant problems we face cannot be solved at the same level of thinking we were at when we created them.*
>
> —*Albert Einstein*

India's civil servants, the new *guardians,* have failed the country. The governance structure, in general, has not performed satisfactorily on most, if not all, relevant considerations. The elements of good governance were summed up well in the *Human Development Report, 1997,* by the United Nations Development Program (UNDP) thus: people's participation, rule of law, transparency, responsiveness, consensus orientation in decision making, equity, effectiveness and efficiency, accountability, and strategic vision. That the scores in India on these criteria have been low is acknowledged widely.

There is a thus a clear and urgent need to improve India's governance. However, we should look at the issues dispassionately — examining the bureaucratic *system* rather than looking at individual bureaucrats. Civil services work within a system where politicians are ruling (and rightly so, in a democracy), but ruling badly. True, some bureaucrats are inefficient, uncaring, and dishonest to boot, but the malaise is omnipresent in Indian society; a large number of industrialists and businessmen are corrupt and so are many professionals, farmers, shopkeepers, craftsmen, mechanics, or *taxiwallahs.*[1] Therefore, let us not pick unnecessarily on civil servants alone.

Babudom has now become a pejorative synonym for bureaucracy. Politician demagogues blame babus for hampering the country's progress and the public blames them for not providing services, but all this is part of a bigger problem. Our emphasis should be not only on reforming the bureaucratic structure and its functioning, but also on improving the working of our political parties and their leaders, and of all legislative bodies. Elected political leaders, after all, are the key players in a democracy — they are supposed to lead and they determine the parameters, providing overall guidance to civil servants. Obviously, bringing back the cherished values of honesty and dedication to the sphere of politics will have a salutary effect on the conduct of bureaucrats and on society at large.

Before reiterating major proposals made for the much-needed bureaucratic reforms for the 21st Century, attention may be drawn to a welcome development on the Indian scene that lends optimism with regard to the country's future. This should counter-balance to some extent the pessimism emanating from a considerable array of negative features of governance — the recurrent theme of this book. The heartening development pertains to people's initiatives in the face of official apathy. Despite the unsatisfactory role of the state, the country is making progress in a number of areas, though at a considerably slower pace than could be achieved in the light of its endowment of resources — human and material. The economy is expanding, actually at a very good pace during recent years. As they say about Italy: The economy grows at night while the government is sleeping! And, people are, by themselves, creating facilities that usually lie in the public sector domain. Gurcharan Das comments on this phenomenon in a recent article in the *Foreign Affairs* journal: "It is an amazing spectacle to see prosperity beginning to spread in today's India even in the presence of appalling governance...Indians despair over the lack of simplest public goods...Today Indians believe that their bureaucracy has become a prime obstacle to development, blocking instead of shepherding economic reform." Das praises the *entrepreneurs' initiatives* and perseverance in the context of rising GDP, and *the people's own initiatives* in the services sector (private schools, healthcare facilities, etc. — the private sector solutions). "India's greatness lies in its self-reliant and resilient people. They are able to pull themselves up and survive, even flourish, when the state fails to deliver."[2]

To come back to our main focus — civil service reforms — the major proposals made in earlier chapters are summarized below:

- Give recognition to technocrats/specialists[3] as extended — in ample measure — to *generalist* civil servants (members of the IAS and Allied Services and of Provincial Civil Services); this can be achieved easily by opening up promotional channels to technocrats/specialists that are currently denied to them and by granting them parity, requisite powers, and financial rewards.

- Establish additional, technical/specialized All-India Services (medical and public health, engineering, agriculture, science and technology, etc.) to be manned by technically qualified people (technocrats/specialists) and not by non-technical regular bureaucrats. The financial and non-monetary rewards available to these technocrats should be fully comparable to those enjoyed by members of the IAS and Allied Services. Then the technical people (doctors, engineers, agricultural scientists, etc.) — trained for long periods at considerable cost to the government — will naturally stay in their own specialized disciplines in preference to joining the generalist services like the IAS where, admittedly and most unfortunately, their specialized training is not utilized.
- Induct more, qualified and experienced, outsiders (from academia, industry, NGOs, etc. including experts from abroad — NRIs and PIOs) at middle and senior levels of civil services. This, for instance, was done by Prime Minister Rajiv Gandhi who invited Sam Pitroda from the United States to improve the telecom structure. Earlier, Pandit Jawahar Lal Nehru had recruited outstanding public men and women (also some from among the rulers of princely states — large and small) on a noticeable scale for India's Foreign Service.
- Increase slightly the number of political appointees in specialized positions where specialized knowledge/ experience is needed and policy content of responsibilities is high. These posts would fall between the level of ministers and the upper echelons of bureaucracy, and would be new and/or created by converting some senior or upper middle level posts of the civil service. Such appointees will, of course, not belong to the civil service.
- End the near-monopoly of the IAS on important posts and the accompanying powers and privileges. The above four suggestions, if followed, would ensure the achievement of this objective.
- Encourage interchange of personnel between academia, public/private sector units, and civil services.
- Improve accountability, efficiency, and responsiveness of

bureaucracy. New personnel policy measures should be tried, e.g. recruiting bureaucrats for short periods — on contracts that could be renewed when deemed necessary or desirable.

Jayaprakash Narain of Loksatta (a member of the Second Administrative Reforms Commission) refers to our system of accountability as 'delightfully vague.' He explains: "Authority almost never goes with responsibility. As a result, we have victims of misgovernance, but no villains!"[4]

- Control corruption through streamlining administrative procedures, introducing transparency, and taking other suitable measures; *freedom of information* is a valuable tool in this regard.
- Remove elitism from civil services and make bureaucracy more service-oriented and courteous.
- Eliminate undue political control and unnecessary political interference in day-to-day administrative activities.
- End reservations in employment, using affirmative action instead wherever justified.
- Reduce significantly the size of our mammoth bureaucracy — exercise girth control. In some areas posts have been reduced over the years due partly to the pressure put by international financial institutions, but such reductions have not been adequate. Despite growing needs to provide public services to ever-increasing population, it should be possible to phase out a large number of jobs in a majority of government departments. However, such decisions should be based on a case-by-case consideration. Some departments/sections/other official entities may well need larger staff, rather than smaller, in view of the nature of their responsibilities, e.g. intelligence gathering and anti-terrorism activities in general.

Contracting out some services would aid in achieving the goal of a smaller bureaucracy. Computerization and utilization of other appropriate equipment and gadgets can help significantly in cutting down the size of bureaucracy while improving operational efficiency. The government should use the latest technologies, particularly the IT, for streamlining bureaucracy and for providing government services online wherever possible.

At present India holds a low rank of 87 in the world in E-governance readiness. According to the *U.N. Global E-governance Readiness Report 2005: From E-government to E-inclusion*, India's E-governance readiness is 0.4001 compared with the world average of 0.4267 in 2005. This assessment is based on a composite index comprising web measure, infrastructure, and human capital assessment. The U.S. leads the 2005 global E-governance readiness rankings, as it did in the previous years, with the highest index of 0.9062 followed closely by Denmark, Sweden, and the United Kingdom. Among developing countries, the Republic of Korea (0.8727) leads, with Singapore, Estonia, Malta, and Chile slightly behind.

According to the report, although India slipped one point in the relative ranking in 2005, it nevertheless reinforced its offerings. The report talked about India's notable contributions in online participation, e.g. through the portal on Government Policies. Another government site that got a mention was of the Department of Administrative Reforms and Public Grievances; this site enables users to lodge a complaint about an issue that was not resolved through the regular administrative procedure of the agency in question and to track the status of the grievance lodged.[5]

With regard to downsizing, Maharashtra's Administrative Reforms Commission, for instance, had recommended in 2003 a five per cent cut in posts at all levels of the administrative hierarchy. The bureaucracy in the state, as elsewhere in India, is huge and decidedly top-heavy.[6] Examples of huge departmental bureaucracies, of course, abound in other states of India as well.

The top-heavy bureaucratic structure in India has changed the organizational *pyramid* into more of a *cylinder* and if the trend continues we will soon have an *inverted pyramid!* Heedless upgrading of posts through cadre reviews is certainly an undesirable practice. A large number of posts should be eliminated right away in the interest of economy and productivity. In this connection, there used to be a law in Japan setting *Total Staff Numbers* under which staff ceilings were reviewed and reported to the parliament for reduction. We should consider enacting similar legislation, and utilize *zero-base budgeting* and other measures to ensure that useless posts and departments get axed unceremoniously.

In addition to slimming the gargantuan administrative apparatus, trimming the size of the ministries to the recommended 10 per cent of the legislators' strength in the lower house (a recommendation that has been honoured more in breach than in observance) would be highly desirable. In many states, all — or almost all — MLAs are made ministers or chairpersons of some government/quasi-government body. Shouldn't the politicians set a good example by limiting the size of ministries before they start reducing the size of the bureaucracy? *Charity should begin at home!*

Incidentally, the Fifth Pay Commission had recommended slashing the government workforce by 30 per cent, abolishing 350,000 vacant posts, and reducing the number of pay scales from 51 to 34. However, these sensible suggestions were never implemented. Similar was the fate of the Commission's recommendation that the grant of salary hikes to employees be linked to issues of downsizing the government, efficiency, and administrative reforms. The implementation of the recommendations actually related only to pay raises! Consequently, the wage bill of the central government alone shot up to about 436 billion Rupees in 1999-2000 from some 219 billions in 1996-1997 — an increase of 99 per cent. The wage bill of state governments rose by 74 per cent, to approximately 898 billion Rupees. No wonder almost 90 per cent of the states' revenues is going towards paying salaries. The impact of the Fifth Pay Commission was so brutal that 13 states did not have money to pay salaries in 2000!

Not surprisingly, the World Bank had held the Fifth Pay Commission as 'the single largest shock to India's strained public finances,' but this has not deterred the government from setting up the Sixth Pay Commission. The prime minister had actually been talking about it for some time, saying in early 2006 that "the time has now come for a new Commission."[7] But, raising salaries without implementing other reforms would be tantamount to inviting certain financial disaster.

However, downsizing of the bureaucracy should be done in a way that recognizes the basic rights of the employees; they should not be made to pay the price of re-inventing the government. There are several ways in which the desired goals can be reached. Besides the obvious use of attrition (retirements and resignations and — in rare cases in India — removal from service), other suggestions include:

— Offer employees severance packages or early retirement incentives (the so-called *golden handshake*).

— Shift dislocated employees to other government jobs and to public sector undertakings.
— Help in finding jobs in the private sector, through out-placement services.
— Provide assistance in retraining the employees, as necessary.
— Require employers in private sector companies, if and when government jobs are contracted to them, to take in the dislocated bureaucrats. David Osbourne and Peter Plastrik give an example of civil service managers taking their local government department/section outside, forming a private entity.[8]

While action is planned on desirable reforms indicated above — working out details and expediting implementation — some steps should be taken, *outright*, in selected areas to convey the intended seriousness. A clear message should be sent out that the government means business and that the measures being taken are not *token* actions but form vanguard of an incipient and potent reform movement. Here are some suggestions for *immediate* action:

- *Appoint technocrats as Secretaries of four or five additional technical departments at the Centre and in the States* — in Medical and Public Health, Agriculture, Forestry, Science and Technology, etc. — as the first installment. Some technical departments at the Centre do have technocrats working as Secretaries, e.g. the Department of Agricultural Research, Extension, and Education, and of Biotechnology. In states where even directors of technical departments are IAS/PCS officers[9], the practice should be discontinued and technocrats placed in those posts. This overdue recognition of the value and relevance of technically qualified people in the emerging, development-oriented environment is bound to speed up economic progress in India.
- *Take some eminent people — say, a dozen or so to begin with — at senior levels, from outside the civil service, to man key positions.* They will become regular bureaucrats. After all, we do have people like Dr. Manmohan Singh who came to the senior echelons of the civil service after doing outstanding work outside. Dr. Singh later joined politics, becoming Finance Minister and now, as you know, he is the

Prime Minister.[10] Surely, there are some experts like him, working somewhere, who may seek — or may be persuaded to serve the nation in — senior bureaucratic positions. They would certainly bring fresh ideas to the system and encourage others to try new approaches. Their examples are bound to create competitive pressures — goading existing bureaucrats to improve their performance.

- *Develop and enforce a fair transfer policy to provide security of tenure,* say for two or three years, so the civil servant can concentrate on work (and not on packing and unpacking — sometimes every *few* months).
- *Introduce transparency in government operations,* in selected areas to start with. At the district level, some departments are dens of wholesale corruption. In one district in U.P. that the author knows about, the Arms Clerk used to be transferred every few months so that every clerk got an equal chance to extort money from applicants for new licenses for weapons or for renewals. What a perversely equitable treatment of thuggish officials and horrendous treatment of members of the public! It should not be difficult to do official business openly. Senior officials should ensure that criteria for requests and entitlements are publicized and the list of applicants for licenses and permissions, etc., and of cases approved, are put on the notice board — especially in all important areas where bureaucrats regularly deal with the public and exercise discretionary powers.[11] Let the government immediately choose a few offices to be set right.
- *Extend protection to whistle-blowers and to those who dare to do the right thing;* many individuals of integrity and with passion for service have done wonders, often single-handedly. T.N. Seshan brought about, as Chief Election Commissioner, some much-needed reforms in the electoral process. In Kerala, V.J. Kurian (also an IAS officer) fought undue pressure from higher-ups when he was working at the Cochin airport. As a result of his hard work and obdurate refusal to play by the usual rules of the game, Cochin now has a clean and efficient international airport — a world-class facility. Unlike most other airports in India, it also makes a profit! But Kurian had to negotiate an assault course of hurdles to achieve this. The case is described in some detail in a recent

insightful book on India by Edward Luce (to which reference has been made earlier) in Chapter 2, "The Burra Sahibs: The Long Tentacles of India's State." Luce quotes Kurian: "The most difficult moment was when I was called by a very senior politician…[who] wanted me to choose the second lowest bidder for the contract to build the airport runway and that I should discard the lowest bidder. When I said I would not break the rules, he said there was one crore (ten million) rupees (over 200,000 dollars) in it for me. I stood my ground. The politician did not know what to say!" Kurian also made this observation about bureaucracy: "When I talk to left-wing friends [there are many in his state, Kerala], I tell them they have got it so wrong — the true exploiter class in India is the bureaucracy…they live off the people. They are your exploiters…If you look at the new recruits to the IAS they are worse than my generation. They want money right away…That is why it is getting worse."[12]

At the State level, there was one PCS officer in U.P. — Hardev Singh *Baba* — who, as Municipal Commissioner in Ghaziabad, had many unauthorized buildings and shopping complexes (constructed on public land, without obtaining title or permission) razed to the ground; he became a holy terror to scoff-laws in the town (kudos to him!) but soon he had to pay a price — *you probably guessed it*: transfer to a post (Director of the Veterinary Department) where he did not have much scope to punish grabbers and cheaters. What justice — getting punished rather than rewarded for integrity and forcefully enforcing the laws and regulations!

- *Improve accountability of government operations;* select, say four or five of the biggest projects in each state and publish a performance scorecard once a month detailing:
  - the progress in specific, measurable terms against the set targets;
  - the money spent on the project, actual *versus* the budgeted amount; and
  - reasons for shortfalls, if any, and plans to correct the situation.
  - The information should be released to the public, including publication in leading newspapers. The names

of minister(s) and officials responsible for executing each project should be included in the write-up. Such a pilot scheme could, in time, be expanded to cover other projects.

The set of immediate reforms suggested above is *doable*. Necessary action can be taken *administratively* — through simple notifications or ordinances. In a large number of cases affecting personnel, the Prime Minister and the Chief Ministers are empowered to take interim/short-term decisions. In the meanwhile, any needed legislative processes should be set in motion. *Political will, found sorely lacking during recent decades, should be mustered for effecting meaningful reforms.* If this cannot be done, talking about reforms would be hypocritical besides being a complete waste of time.

The measures of a prompt nature just suggested — followed assiduously by action on time-consuming mid- and long-term actions recommended earlier — can take the country on the road to rapid, equitable, and sustainable progress.

It may be added that some of the suggested reform measures could adversely affect service prospects of the existing civil servants, e.g. by limiting promotional opportunities when outsiders are taken at middle and senior levels. This ought to be addressed through short- and long-term compensatory measures to protect the interests of incumbent bureaucrats who entered civil services under a set of expectations. Corrective, short-term measures could, for instance, include: promotions in place; finding suitable placements in the public sector; referrals to the private sector, etc. as indicated earlier in this section. For the long run, the government could *reduce the intake of direct entrants* to broadly preserve the ratio of the promotees to total staff strength. These steps would enable the government to honour the compact — specified or implied — with members of civil services.

It is, however, worth emphasizing that reforming a system — bureaucratic or any other type — is not a final solution in itself. Often, after initial successes (e.g. achieving a smaller size of the civil service) things change. The underlying force (say, the desire to have more power and a bigger staff — the so called *empire-building* urge) reasserts itself. To avoid such relapses, the culture of the system — its *DNA* if you would — ought to be changed for self-perpetuating outcomes. The bureaucratic structure has to be made to shed its inertia and sloth, and acquire in its place an *analytical* and *innovative* spirit.

The resulting bureaucracy will habitually look at its own functioning and engage continually in improving its performance *without having to be pushed from outside*. It is really all about building an entrepreneurial-minded civil service with a built-in drive to improve, so as to become *self-renewing*.

Soon after taking over as prime minister, Manmohan Singh had indicated that bureaucratic reform would be a high priority of his government. This declaration of intent and a few preliminary actions announced by him shortly after taking over reminded one of the swift and forceful moves made by the prime minister of the U.K., Margaret Thatcher (*the Iron Lady*), who came to power in the winter of 1979, pledging to revive the country's slumping economy — by, among other things, reducing the size of, and reforming, the big bureaucracy. At her very *first* cabinet meeting, Thatcher announced a hiring freeze and a three-per cent cut in the civil service; several months later, she imposed an additional five-per cent cut. On her *fourth* day in office, she appointed Sir Derek Rayner (head of the Marks & Spencer retail chain) to lead a crusade against waste and inefficiency. In the 18 years after Prime Minister Thatcher launched bureaucratic and economic reforms, the U.K. government succeeded in shrinking its civil service by as much as 33 per cent, using a variety of techniques, and with only few layoffs![13]

That the Indian prime minister was serious about improving the nation's governance became obvious when the government set up the Second Administrative Reforms Commission (SARC) in mid-2005 — giving it a wide mandate. Indications are that the group is hard at work; its term, which was due to end on 31st August 2006, was extended in mid-July by one year — through August 31, 2007. The panel certainly has a very difficult and complex task at hand. One would naturally wish to extend sincere, best wishes to the Chairman, members, and staff of the Commission for successful completion of the highly worthwhile and long-overdue venture to reform the country's bureaucracy.

After the SARC has submitted its report, two sets of questions would arise relating to:

- the coverage, quality of the work, and the feasibility of the recommendations made by the panel; and
- action by the government to carry out reforms in the light of its administrative competence, and more importantly, the

political will to take bold steps (directly and through legislative measures).

The latter category may pose serious difficulties, as forceful political action has not been possible in recent decades, e.g. in executing reforms recommended by the National Police Commission. Political compulsions and the leaders' strong reluctance to give up their powers to misuse the bureaucratic machinery have indeed been insurmountable hurdles. Political timidity and narrow considerations (catering to the demands of 'vote banks,' for example) have been the hallmarks of political behaviour for many years.

Lack of numerical legislative strength of individual political parties has resulted in many a patchwork, coalition government. In such cases, given lower than sterling standards of political conduct, governments became hostage to political blackmail, bickering, and horse-trading; political inaction has been the natural outcome. In fact, the nation now seems to have become immune to realizing the magnitude of the harm that narrow, short-term political interests are causing.

The limited degree of freedom to act available to the present Congress-led coalition has also been commented upon by some leading Western observers. Thus, Scott Baldauf of the *Christian Science Monitor,* a leading U.S. Daily, writes: "Some observers say Mr. [Manmohan] Singh's greatest achievement [so far] maybe simply staying in office. Surrounded by leftist coalition supporters who oppose almost every economic reform, and right-wing opposition parties who [at times] refuse to attend parliament, Singh is an isolated figure…Modestly, Singh himself gives his government's first year in office a barely passing grade of 6 out of 10."[14] The London *Economist,* in a mid-December 2006 Special Report, commented on the government's move to retract a sensible policy decision: "Worst of all, Indian politics may actually be retreating to its bureaucratic past. Take oil pricing, a complex statist rigmarole that had been moving from the hands of government to those of a regulator: Under Mr. Singh [the Prime Minister], price decisions are again being taken by the government." *The Economist* also refers to the Prime Minister's instincts being 'depressingly bureaucratic' sometimes. "Faced with obvious and long-standing problems, he commissions a study on them."[15]

It is imperative that India's political leaders, senior bureaucrats, and others who lay down/influence/execute policies rose above partisanship and their short-term narrow agendas, and acted with vigour and promptness in translating the SAARC's recommendations that are considered meritorious. That should, with luck, go a long way towards ensuring that the country has in place a governance structure that is specialized, efficient, honest, and responsive. Only then could India become a fully developed country and take its rightful place in the comity of nations — a deserved claimant to the super-power status. It is hoped this golden opportunity to reform bureaucracy will not be missed and the government proves wrong the statement made by an astute observer of the Indian scene: "India never misses an opportunity to miss an opportunity!"

ENDNOTES

CHAPTER I

1. Bureaucracy may be defined as an organizational structure characterized by assigned functions, hierarchy, division of responsibility, set procedures, and impersonal relationships. That such an administrative structure is necessary for the government — even on the smallest of scales — to administer its programmes and implement its policies is indisputable.
2. The Egyptian king was the supreme head of state. Next to him, the most powerful officer was the *vizier* — executive head of the bureaucratic system. His title translates as "Superintendent of all Works of the King". The hierarchical structure and code of ethics of the Egyptian bureaucracy are echoed in modern governments. See *Egyptian Civilization: Government.* http:www.civilization.cacivilEgyptegcgov3e.html
3. By contrast, until the British rule administrative posts in India were mostly hereditary — filled by select castes, a significant proportion being Brahmins; Kayasthas also became choice appointees during the Mughal days, in particular. In the army, martial castes predominated — even more so during the British days.
4. For an authentic description of the ICS see *The Men Who Ruled India: The Guardians* by Philip Mason, published by:

   W.W. Norton & Co., Inc., First Abridged American Edition, 1985.

   Pan Macmillan, Paperback Edition, 1987.

   Rupa & Co., New Delhi, Abridged Edition, 1992.
5. Nehru even persuaded the last British viceroy, Lord Mounbatten, to remain as the first head of state of Independent India.
6. "The Iron Man Forged the Steel Frame of India" (Extracts from B. Krishna's book, *Sardar Vallabh Bhai Patel: India's Iron Man), The News India Times* (Weekly), New York, November 29, 1996.
7. "The ICS and I", *The Illustrated Weekly of India,* June 21, 1964; this was part of a series of informative and very readable articles written by seven leading civil servants, published in the *IW* during April-November, 1964.
8. "The End of the Empire", in *Adventures of Mind,* Edited by Richard Thruelsen and John Kobler, Alfred A. Knopf, New York, 1960, p. 132.

9. The annual growth target for the 11th Five-Year Plan (2007–2012) is put at 10 per cent (towards final years of the Plan), "to set our economy on the growth path which would finally liberate millions of our countrymen from the perennial scourges of poverty, ignorance and diseases," in the words of Prime Minister Manmohan Singh.
10. According to Shashi Tharoor, the dividing lines between the rich and poor in India, and between eastern and western countries are "the high-speed digital optical fiber lines!"
11. Suman Guha Mozumdar, "India needs $1.5 trillion for Great Economic Leap," *India Abroad* (Weekly), New York, October 6, 2006, p. A-24.
12. Aziz Haniffa, "Largest-ever Trade Mission Prepares for India Trip," *India Abroad* (Weekly), New York, December 1, 2006, p. A-24.
13. "The ICS and I," *Op Cit.*
14. "Volunteers of America: Four Youngsters Narrate Their Real Encounters with India," *India Abroad* (Weekly), New York, November 17, 2006.
15. *Hamlet,* Act I, Sc. 4, "Something is rotten in the State of Denmark."
16. *Wings of Fire: An Autobiography,* Universities Press, Hyderabad, AP, India, 2003 (15th edition), p. 76.
17. Some examples:

    Charles Dickens: "Bureaucracy…skewered through and through with office-pens, and bound hand and foot with red tape."

    James Boren: "Bureaucrats are the only people in the world who can say absolutely nothing and mean it."

    Honoré de Balzac: "Bureaucracy is a giant mechanism operated by pygmies."

    Javier Pascal Salcedo: "Bureaucracy is the art of making the possible impossible."

    Bureaucracy has been referred to as *Bureaucrazy* by M.M. Kaw, a senior member of the IAS, who has written a humorous book of that title. Some Latin Americans call bureaucracy *Burrocracy!* (*Burro* is a donkey in Spanish.)

    See http:www.quotemeonit.combureaucracy.html and *Bartlett's Quotations.*
18. S.N. Chary, "Civil Services: Total Revamping Needed", *The Indian Express,* June 9, 1995.
19. Interview of B.K. Chaturvedi by Naresh Taneja: "Too Much Procedure Means Corruption," *The Times of India,* August 29, 2004.
20. "Bureaucracy: Missionary Service or Mercenary?" *The Hindustan Times,* July 1, 1996.
21. "Civil Services: Total Revamping Needed," *Op Cit.*

22. I had the pleasure of discussing development and civil service issues with Dharma Vira and Khub Chand (both had also served as ambassadors) during their visits to the United States and during my home-leave trips to, and my later political appointments in, India. Dr. M.S. Randhawa, a scientist/ administrator, held the post of Secretary (Agriculture) at the Centre — among many important assignments (including vice chancellorship of Punjab Agricultural University at Ludhiana after his retirement from the civil service) — and it was very useful to discuss with him policy aspects of agricultural development and the administrative structure for extension services. He, as well as S. Tarlok Singh — Member-Secretary of the Planning Commission — were administrators with a pronounced academic/analytical bent of mind that made their views specially valuable. Tarlok Singh wrote one of the first good books on economic development in India, *Poverty and Social Change,* followed by several other works. On my return to India in the mid-1980s we re-established contact. I persuaded him to deliver the 1988 Sir Chhotu Ram Memorial Lecture on Rural Development at CCS-Haryana Agricultural University. During his visit I, and many faculty members, benefited from the intimate knowledge of this pioneering thinker on planning for economic & social advancement and on the role of bureaucracy. He as well as Dr. M.S. Randhawa articulated very well the connection between civil services and development. Another person I exchanged views with was M.G. Kaul who was posted as Minister (Econ.) in our Embassy in Washington, D.C., during my early days with an international organization, which I had joined in 1965. We had occasions to discuss international economic affairs, especially in areas where these intersected with India's interests, and latest developments in India affecting economic growth. With Bhagwan Singh (who had been selected for the ICS but — since the British were leaving India around that time — was absorbed in the IAS; he, too, had served as ambassador to Fiji) discussions on India's problems, especially poverty and deprivation, lack of progress, and needed reforms in civil services were recurrent themes — pursued mainly after my return to India. I found that T.N. Kaul (also of the ICS, who had served as foreign secretary and as India's ambassador to the United States) held particularly strong views on the need for bureaucratic reforms.

23. However, I did not have an editor/manuscript reader of the kind that a U.S. Chief of Army Staff used to have. The story was told years ago by a professor of statistics when we were discussing in a sampling course the need for framing survey questions that are clear, simple, and succinct; it went like this: The top general in the Pentagon had a staff aide, a captain, whom the general wanted to promote to the major's rank. The colonel handling personnel matters objected, saying that the staff aide — not terribly bright to begin with, just set in his office all day and read the army manuals and circulars going to the G.I.s, the lowest ranks, in the field. This was the sole duty of the aide who has had the distinction of being awarded the title

"goat" at his graduation from the U.S. Military Academy at West Point; that title is reserved for the cadet who graduates at the bottom rank in his batch! The colonel's considered advice was to wait before granting a promotion. But the general was insistent, saying that the staff aide rendered highly valuable and unique service to the U.S. Armed Forces: "If he can understand the language/contents of the manuals and circulars — as drafted or after suitable modifications desired by him — then the dumbest soldier in the field, too, would understand what the instructions were!

CHAPTER II

1. Max Weber has probably been the most influential user of the word; however, *bureaucracy* was an English word in use before Weber was even born, appearing in the Oxford Dictionary in different years between 1818 and 1860.
   http:www.free-definition.comBureaucracy.html
2. "Towards a Bamboo Frame," Mani Talk, *Sunday,* February 19-25, 1995.
3. "The ICS and I," *The Illustrated Weekly of India,* November 1, 1964.
4. "Civil Servants: Serving the Master," *The Indian Express,* August 25, 1995.
5. B. Krishna, "The Iron Man Forged the Steel Frame of India," *Op Cit.*
6. See http:www.deesha.orgarchives20040409.
7. He, of course, feels we should develop economically but points out a special feature of our poverty by quoting Ambassador John Kenneth Galbraith who had seen poverty in many countries of the world but found one unusual attribute among the poor of India: "There is richness in their poverty." They may have no *standard of living* but still have a *standard of life* is Palkhivala's interpretation. He adds: "The ancient civilization has survived and will survive when the raucous and fractious voices of today are lost in the silence of the centuries."
8. "The Intricate Art of Indecision," *The Indian Express,* March 19, 2004.
9. Some officers of Pondicherry Administration of those days and faculty members of Pondicherry Central University with whom I had interacted closely, remain in touch to this day.
10. Our significant achievements included: full adult literacy — the second State/UT in the nation to meet this goal (Kerala being the first) — in recognition of which we received the *King Sezong Award for Literacy* from UNESCO; higher educational achievements — at Pondicherry University (the Governor is the honorary Chief Rector of the university) and in different colleges — and holding a very successful *International Conference on Experiential Learning;* new initiatives in improving environment and ecology; development of tourism; promotion of arts and culture, including the setting up of an *Art Gallery* in the Raj Niwas; and beautifying

Pondicherry and three other regions of the U.T. — Karaikal in Tamil Nadu, Mahé in Kerala, and Yanam in Andhra Pradesh. All this tended to make Pondicherry a model UT/State.

I also thought it would be a good idea to put two guns, one on each side, of the main gate of the Raj Niwas as part of improving the environs aesthetically. We unearthed one gun and borrowed another from the police offices' compound. All of the governors' mansions (Raj Bhavan/Raj Niwas) that I had seen displayed such guns and our French-built, impressive Raj Niwas seemed also in need of them. The installation, *sans* fanfare, was received very well except for a few stray comments about my initiative being a throw back to the feudal/colonial days!

11. "Bureaucracy Bashing," *The Times of India,* May 14, 1997.

CHAPTER III

1. Loksatta — Corruption Eradication Paper, Rediff Home Pages, September 16, 2004.
   http//www.members. Rediff.comcorruption_eradicationtentofourteen.htm
2. I once heard a story about such a *bureaucrat* agricultural officer whose knowledge about nitrates was limited to ni(gh)trates being lower than day rates!
3. "IAS — Highly Overrated," *The Hindustan Times,* December 22, 1995.
4. "Premier Bodies Remain Headless," *The Indian Express,* August 6, 1995.
5. "Development: Change the Tools", *The Pioneer,* September 25, 1999.
6. "Civil Service after Independence," *World Affairs,* December 1994.
7. For the job of registrar, CCS-Haryana Agricultural University (HAU) has actually taken on deputation several IAS officers. But many universities, feeling that an academic background would be helpful even in management jobs, routinely choose professors or heads of departments/deans to work as registrars; apparently, they enjoy greater confidence of faculty members. Thus, the current registrar at HAU — Prof. Randhir Singh Dalal — is an academic: a reputed agricultural extension expert, teacher, and human resources development expert; he also served as a competent P.S. during my tenure as a Member of the Planning Commission at New Delhi, which exposed him to national policy issues. This type of specialist is needed for administrative work in the universities of today where specialized issues — e.g. international exchange of scientists and students, and collaborative research projects — require subject matter knowledge. Incidentally, HAU recently signed a Memorandum of Understanding for broad collaboration with the University of Maryland in the United States and is actively exploring the possibility of entering into a similar agreement with North Carolina State University.

8. My immediate predecessor at CCS-Haryana Agricultural University belonged to the IAS, and while the search was on for a new person, another IAS officer held interim charge for six months or so before I could wind up my affairs in the United States and join the university. I saw no reason why a serving senior Dean or Director — out of many competent ones — could not have been appointed as a stopgap measure. Obviously, civil service is not the preferred/appropriate background to have for heading an academic institution — and not at all for an agricultural university or a technical institute (IIT and others).
9. At one time, Mr. Narayanan had also served as India's Ambassador to the United States.
10. The inter-governmental agency I worked for was housed in the USDA's South Building for over two decades and this facilitated constant interaction with the department's employees — from the Foreign Agricultural Service, Economic Research Service, Agricultural Stabilization and Conservation Service, Agricultural Research Service, etc. — who were all true professionals, *specialists* in their fields, with a significant number holding doctorate degrees.
11. One exception I know of was Dr. M.S. Swaminathan, the well-known agricultural scientist, who served as secretary of the main agriculture department.
12. In Kashmir a rift was reported over this policy between members of the IAS and IPS. The government had ordered in 1995 that the ACRs of police officers would be written by IAS officers. Thus, the divisional commissioners were to write the reports of the inspectors general of police (IGPs). It was pointed out that in the Jammu region the divisional commissioner, an IAS officer, was four years junior to the IGP, and the police officers found it 'totally unfair' that an IAS officer would be assessing the IGP's performance. In fact, the state government had tried this policy once earlier also — but had to withdraw it soon after police officers lodged strong protests. See M.L. Kak, "IAS-IPS Rift over Policy", *The Tribune,* April 11, 1995.
13. An example of discrimination against competent technocrats relates to a distant cousin of mine — Bhupal Singh — a brilliant professional, who had graduated from the top engineering institute of the time (Thompson Engineering College, Roorke — now a university, included in the world-renowned IIT system). He had gone up to the top position in his field — Chief Engineer (Electricity) in Uttar Pradesh (U.P.) — and was later made a Member of the U.P. Electricity Board but could not be named its chairman. That post — by tradition or encadrement — was reserved for an IAS officer. When the V.P. Singh government came to power at the Centre in 1989-end and Mulayam Singh Yadav became the State's Chief Minister, Bhupal Singh did get appointed chairman, but only after some hassles.

14. The marriage market in India calculates — in the best tradition of market economics — the economic and social content of the premium that members of elite civil services command. There is a perfect correlation between the notorious wedding dowry and the groom's service prospects, with members of the IAS and Allied Services coming on top, followed by doctors/engineers/other technical people. Then come other government servants as they, too, enjoy complete job security. Employees in the private sector were not regarded as choice catches until recently when very high salaries and productive, hassle-free work environment — in the wake of expanded economic opportunities, rapid industrial progress, the IT Revolution, and globalization — boosted their position substantially.
15. Charulata Joshi, "The New Power-Baggers," *New India Digest,* No. 31, November-December, 1992, p. 57.
16. "Have B.E., Will Get into IAS," *The Tribune,* September 11, 1993.
17. "Steel Frame of Bureaucracy Rusting," *News India Times* (Weekly), New York, August 22, 1997.
18. Interview of B.K. Chaturvedi by Naresh Taneja: "Too Much Procedure Means Corruption," *The Times of India,* September 16, 2004.
19. I know several officers who entered the Service with the minimum academic background. Taking some high-scoring subjects like mathematics and Sanskrit reportedly helps in competitive examinations in comparison to many other subjects that would be more directly useful from the point of view of the civil servant's value to society. The examination system could be improved, I presume, to take into account — and make adjustment for — the marks-scoring potential of different subjects.
20. To give an idea of such outlays, Haryana Agricultural University's annual budget in the late-1980s was in excess of $20 million — a huge sum for an Indian University, especially when seen in terms of its *purchasing power parity;* the budgets of the usual arts/sciences universities were substantially smaller.
21. With our advice and some help, more students started succeeding in competitive examinations for the IAS and Allied Services. The successful candidates appreciated our limited but tactical support, and a few of them kept in touch with me for years. However, I have often wondered whether extending our help was the right thing to do.
22. "Varsities Should Evolve IAS-oriented Syllabus," *The Hindu,* May 30, 1993 and Suresh Nambath, "Universities To Introduce Foundation Course," *The Indian Express,* July 4, 1995.
23. "D.U. Boy Tops Civil Service Exam," *The Hindustan Times,* June 18, 1996.
24. With regard to placing people in jobs best suited to their qualifications, there is a joke doing the rounds in our Foreign Service: If you wish to avoid posting to a particular country, learn the language spoken there — learn Mandarin and you will never be posted to China!

25. My father didn't like my move, maintaining that I would be working for *Banias* — businessmen/traders/industrialists (in preference to my erstwhile employers/mentors — economists of world fame, Prof. V.K.R.V. Rao and Dr. P.S. Lokanathan). However, my father's disappointment slowly melted away when he saw that — besides being paid well — I was very happy in what I was doing in a productive, supportive, and congenial environment provided by the progressive management of a company which was contributing noticeably — along with others — towards job creation and the country's overall economic development.

26. While academic people do enjoy respect in some circles, civil servants in the secretariats and elsewhere often are not accommodating to their needs and specific, justified requests. At a Vice Chancellors' Annual Meeting references to this matter were made by several respected academics in the context of red tape and general foot-dragging; in a few cases, a deputy secretary or joint secretary showed arrogance in not even receiving the vice chancellor with courtesy. Since the universities depend on state and central governments for funds and other support, bureaucratic dilatory tactics and non-cooperation adversely affect the functioning of academic institutions. Vice chancellors are rated by the government at the level of central additional secretary/secretary but, generally speaking, the bureaucrats — especially many of those at senior levels — are not all that impressed by academic people! Gone are the days when vice chancellors were respected *everywhere* — not just on the campus. It is said that Prime Minister Nehru had, on occasions called on the heads of Benares Hindu University (Pandit Madan Mohan Malaviya and others) *at their university residences.* In Hindu scriptures, the teacher (*guru*) is put right after God as deserving of reverence, but try telling that to a functionary in th0e secretariat!

CHAPTER IV

1. "Can We Improve Public Service Delivery?" September 10, 2005. http:www.financialexpress.com
2. "Time To Close the IAS Shop?" *The Hindustan Times,* July 2, 1995.
3. The Indian Economic Service was set up after a lot of serious grumbling by economists serving in the government; a prominent, highly qualified economist working at a senior level, for instance, complained vociferously (and proceeded on leave) when he was passed over for promotion and an IAS (or an ICS) officer was selected.
4. In Haryana, the case of an able Chief Conservator of Forests was informally recommended to the Chief Minister by a couple of senior technocrats, for appointment as Secretary to the State's Forest Department. However, it was not considered since the post was encadred (reserved) for a member of the IAS; such encadrement is the usual practice. The C.M. was advised by

senior bureaucrats not to move for decadrement of any such post. The person who came over from the Centre to take over as Secretary of the Forest Department had been — if I remember correctly — with a department/council in New Delhi dealing with women's social welfare.

5. I had participated a number of times in senior-level selections, as a co-opted outside expert, and was impressed by the quality of work being done by the ASRB.
6. *My Years Through Raj to Swaraj,* Vikas Publishing House Pvt. Ltd, New Delhi, 1993, p. 85.
7. "Advantages of Being in the IAS," *The Indian Express,* September 30, 1995.
8. "Are IAS, IPS Model Services?" *The Hindustan Times,* December 8, 1996.
9. The Tata Administrative Service officers (a large proportion of whom have MBAs from leading business schools) are specialists in management, finance (budgeting and accounting), performance/sector analysis, perspective planning, etc., and they move up to head sections/departments where the use of such expertise is called for. Their presence in the company is not overarching.
10. "Towards a Bamboo Frame," *Op Cit.*
11. The Director of Research at CCS-Haryana Agricultural University handled a big staff and controlled an annual budget of some $10 million in the late 1980s; he did acquire valuable administrative experience — far more, I bet, than many people in regular administrative jobs.
12. "It was a Hermit's Life: Topping Civil Services Was Nirvana," *The Times of India,* June 19, 1996.
13. "The Second Attempt Made all the Difference," *The Hindustan Times,* June 19, 1996.
14. Howard Gardner, *Frames of Mind: The Theory of Multiple Intelligences,* Basic Books, New York, 1983. Gardner also wrote a follow-up book, *Intelligence Reframed: Multiple Intelligences for the 21st Century,* published by the same N.Y. Company in 1999.
15. Justin Pope, "Yale Psychologist Creates Possible Alternative to SATs," *The Examiner* (Daily), Washington, D.C., March 7, 2005.
16. "Emotions Are the Source of Real Intelligence," *The Times of India,* November, 5, 1995 — by arrangement with *The Sunday Times,* London.
17. "Towards a Bamboo Frame," *Op Cit.*

CHAPTER V

1. Such interchange between different sectors/disciplines is commonplace in the United States. Two notable cases of journalists moving to the government

and academia/think-tanks come to mind: Strobe Talbot, a former deputy secretary in the State Department, was a correspondent and columnist for *Time* magazine for over two decades; currently he is president of the Brookings Institution, a prestigious think tank in Washington, D.C. And Karl Inderfurth, who had worked as a T.V. journalist before serving as assistant secretary of state for South Asia, is now a professor of international affairs at George Washington University, also in Washington, D.C.

2. Thus, there have been people like Prof. A.M. Khusro (formerly Director, Institute of Economic Growth in Delhi and Vice Chancellor of Aligarh Muslim University) who held a couple of political appointments — as Member of India's Planning Commission and Ambassador to Germany.
3. "Bringing Competition to Bureaucracy," *The Economic Times,* September 27, 2000.
4. Some are prone to tell even if they did not kiss!
5. I understand that the former External Affairs Minister, Jaswant Singh, had pushed for such secondment of IFS officers to outside agencies but the shortage of people in the Ministry reportedly came in the way of executing his ideas.
6. In the past many of those who were sent to outside agencies on deputation never returned, especially those who went to lucrative assignments with international organizations like the World Bank and the International Monetary Fund.

CHAPTER VI

1. I had the pleasure of knowing one *Nawab* — Jam Saheb Amir Ali Khan, a very big landlord of Sindh, who served as Pakistan's Ambassador to Maldives during the mid-1990s when I was posted there as India's envoy. He proved to be a good diplomat. One of his endearing qualities was the absence of maniacal anti-India lobbying that, unfortunately, has been the staple of some Pakistani diplomats' activities around the world.
2. There are several good universities (e.g., Jawahar Lal Nehru University at Delhi and Pondicherry University) and institutes (e.g., Maulana Abul Kalam Azad Institute of Asian Studies at Kolkata) which are doing good work in the field of international/area studies.
3. To name just one: Salman Khurshid — Oxford-educated, suave, and well-regarded politician — who had served ably as Minister of State for External Affairs in the Narasimha Rao Administration.
4. An appointment of the type of individuals I am talking about was made by the present government, of Ajay Singh as India's Ambassador to Fiji. His qualifications: Served as Member of Parliament from Agra and as a young Union Minister; his great-grandfather and grandfather had worked in Fiji;

his father, Bhagwan Singh, too, had served there (as India's Ambassador); Ajay Singh had lived in Fiji earlier and written (as a journalist) about the country (and about various other places/subjects); and — as if all this was not enough by way of qualifications — his gracious wife, Shiromani, is from Fiji! Thus, he knows the country of his posting, and many of its leading citizens, very well — like perhaps few would know before embarking on a new diplomatic assignment.

5. Diplomatic appointments of outsiders, of course, do not have to be made only at the envoy's level. Taking the case of Fiji again, the Cultural Counselor, Dr. Mahavir Singh, comes from the academic side: He was Director and Professor at Maulana Abul Kalam Azad Institute of Asian Studies at Kolkata; prior to that, he was engaged in teaching and research at Pondicherry University where I got to know about the very good work done by the then young academic.

6. Sociability becomes important simply because diplomats have to spend a noticeable amount of time at social functions, official receptions, and the like. Making small talk is unavoidable. Some diplomats develop a good reserve of stories, anecdotes, and jokes. Thus, the Foreign Minister of Maldives, Hon'ble Fathulla Jameel, can regale you with humorous (and depress you with serious) stories for hours. He has been the country's Foreign Minister for some three decades and has had a lot of time to add to his collection and improve his delivery (which, I was told, was very good to begin with). His collection (unpublished) of jokes seems to surpass printed collections of Bennet Cerf's (*Life of the Party,* etc.) and Khushwant Singh's and also those of *Playboy's!*

7. See Stephen Barr's comprehensive article, "The Federal Diary: Why You Can't Just Run off and Join the Foreign Service," *The Washington Post,* October 24, 2004. The procedures are explained at length on the State Department's Website www.careers.state.gov; the details for the written examination part are available at www.groups.yahoo.comgroupfswe

8. See, for example, Ariana Eunjung Cha "Employers Relying on Personality Tests," *The Washington Post,* May 28, 2005.

9. "Inside the Indian Foreign Service," *U.S. Foreign Service Journal,* October 2002, p. 37.

10. The situation has since been corrected; an important agreement with ASEAN was signed some years ago.

11. "Inside the Indian Foreign Service," *Op Cit,* p. 41.

CHAPTER VII

1. "Never Be Certain," Interview by Chandan Mitra of *The Pioneer,* November 12, 2005.
www.dailypioneer.comcolumnist

2. India News at iVarta.com, April 18, 2005.
www.indiacause.comcolumns01_050418.htm

   Sundaram characterizes the inefficiency in our current system of public administration as multiplication and perpetuation like that of Tubercular Bacilli.

3. *In Spite of the Gods: The Strange Rise of Modern India,* Little, Brown, London, 2006, pp. 72-73.

4. The book got excellent reviews. For instance, in a *Washington Post (Book World)* write-up, Shashi Tharoor (himself an outstanding writer), called the narrative "insightful and engaging…richly evocative of place and mood…sophisticated and sympathetic" and felt that while the author was "tough-minded," he had exercised "invariably sound" judgment in his assessments.

5. According to a Z-TV Nightly News Program broadcast in late November, 2006, the collector of Malkagiri district in Orissa slapped an elderly applicant who had come to see him in connection with some official matter. Reportedly, this was not the first time the mighty collector had slapped someone; drunk with power, he had inflicted this punishment on a police constable once, and also on a driver! In describing the incident, the newscaster was reminded of the earlier imperial rule.

6. *In Spite of the Gods: The Strange Rise of Modern India*, *Op Cit,* p. 16.

7. This situation may have changed.

8. Apparently, the collector is responsible for the performance of district police superintendents as he/she writes their ACRs, but if the law and order situation deteriorates in the district (say, due to a riot of some kind), who would be taken to task, even suspended? *Not* the collector but, most likely, the police superintendent(s) and/or other police officers. The collector reaps the glory for good administration but should things go wrong, the person usually goes scot-free. One hears sometimes reports of suspensions of police superintendents, but seldom that of a collector.

9. At a state-level meeting of engineers in 1989 — for which Haryana Agricultural University at Hisar had allowed the use of its commodious auditorium — a proposal was made to request the chief minister (C.M.) of the state for changing the performance evaluation procedures: letting the regional engineers rather than collectors write the ACRs of district engineers. The C.M., who came to the closing session of the meeting, was persuaded to accept this fair and sensible proposal. But I was told, later on, that either the decision was not carried out or was withdrawn by another C.M.

10. Recently an engineer with 25 years of service told me that when he went to receive a collector (in a western U.P. district), the latter — promptly after alighting from the car and cursory introductions — handed him his fat portfolio to carry!

11. "Vanity, Thy Name Is the Indian Bureaucrat," *The Indian Express,* March 21, 2004.

12. Habibullah served as minister for community affairs in the Indian embassy in Washington, D.C. and as an analyst at a think tank (U.S. Institute of Peace) before going back to Delhi to serve as secretary in a central ministry.

13. Once when I was meeting some people at a guesthouse in Ghaziabad (U.P.), there was commotion outside in the yard. We learned that the divisional commissioner from Meerut was visiting and a guard-of-honour was being arranged for him. Do we really need to extend this honour to a divisional commissioner (joint secretary's rank at the centre)?

14. I remember well what we had decided at the Governors' Annual Conference in 1991, held at the Rashtrapati Bhavan (the President of India's imposing residence-cum-office). At one session, a resolution — initiated by my learned colleague from West Bengal, Prof. Nurul Hasan, and a couple of others (with academic background) — was passed unanimously saying that, within our own territories, we should do away with the guard-of-honour ceremony unless it was for some special occasion, e.g., for a national day function or a national/international meeting. That there is waste of time and resources felt all the governors (including a big Raja, the Goa Governor Bhanu Prakash Singh) in ferrying a police group to the guard-of-honour site. Incidentally, due to financial stringency at the time, the governors also decided to take a ten-per cent cut in their salaries.

15. The governor's car in India carries no license plates (just the national emblem) and within own state/territory it can go through red lights — siren screaming from the pilot car (sometimes even when it is not necessary), with flashing red lights; a police jeep with guards follows the governor's car. No wonder, after retirement, I initially had a little difficulty in driving by myself on Delhi roads as nobody was moving out of my way! Did the fact that, in two other jobs also my car flew a flag and/or had a red light on top add to my sense (at a *sub-conscious* level) of special ownership of the road? Not really, because I happily glided into my new, post-retirement life of a non-VVIP — an ex-excellency!

16. For instance, the recently retired chief of police in Washington, D.C. — an important police jurisdiction in the country — rose from the ranks, starting as constable (called police officer in the United States). The new chief (a lady) also comes from the ranks, rising from officer to sergeant, lieutenant, and to captain/commander. This is the general pattern in the country.

17. A friend working in the medical field in the United States stated in the context of knowing and appreciating the difficulties faced by subordinates: "You'd never find a director of nursing in an American hospital who does not have a nursing degree (R.N., B.S.N, etc.) and has not worked as a floor nurse and hung IU bags herself!"

18. "Every IPS Officer Must Begin His Career as a Constable," interview of Ved Marwah, *The Times of India.* (The publication date on the paper cutting of the article was inadvertently left out; the interview was probably reported in *The TOI* in late May, 1998.)
19. Vinay Pandey, "IAS, IPS May Have Fewer Direct Entrants," *The Times of India,* September 19, 1996.
20. V. Radhika, "DANICS Opposes IAS Dominance," *The Pioneer,* August 26, 1996.
21. Anadi Naik, "India's Bureaucracy," *Mera Bharat Mahan,* The Republic Day Souvenir, January 2005, published jointly by some leading Indian American Community Associations of the Washington, DC Metropolitan Area.

CHAPTER VIII

1. In the Indian army, strict assessment at the level of Major seals the fate of many who would never become Lt. Colonels; further winnowing takes place before one is promoted to the rank of a General.

   In the U.S. State Department, a system of "up and out" is followed. Based on periodic performance reviews, employees who do not receive a good rating and are not judged productive for the rank they have reached are asked to leave.
2. See Stephen Barr, "Civil Service System Begins To Fade Away," Federal Diary, *The Washington Post,* November 7, 2003.
3. Quoted by Al Gore (ex-Vice President of the U.S.), *Common Sense Government Works Better and Costs Less,* Random House, New York, 1995, p. 77.
4. *Ibid,* pp. 94–95.
5. I received a notice from the Controller of Defense Accounts (CDA) to produce a Life Certificate for a past period in connection with the two awards granted to my father for bravery on the front— *Jangi Inam*, and for distinguished army service — *Jagir Allowance,* in lieu of land grant.
6. Quoted by N. Nardi, *Conversation Pieces*, Caravelle Books, New York, 1968, p. 83.
7. The need for this specification arose because a previous vice chancellor whose verbal order was carried out denied later about having given any such instruction. The Hon'ble (?) vice chancellor did so as the action taken in compliance of his order had proved highly controversial.
8. *Memoirs of a Civil servant,* Vikas Publishing House Pvt. Ltd., Delhi, 1975, p. 21.
9. "The ICS and I," *The Illustrated Weekly of India,* July 26, 1964.

10. "A New Administration: Beyond Henry Fordism and the Self-deceiving State," Paper for a Retreat (11-12 December, 1989) arranged by the Institute of Development Studies, University of Sussex, U.K.; Administrative Staff College, Hyderabad.
11. Banglapedia: Curzon, Lord, September 17, 2004. http:www.search.com. bdbanglapediaContentHTC-0391.HTM
12. "Filing the State Away", Address at the India Today Conclave, *The Indian Express,* March 18, 2004.
13. *Governance and the Sclerosis That Has Set In,* Rupa & Co, New Delhi, 2004, pp. 3-7.
14. "Filing the State Away," *Op Cit.*
15. "World Bank Finds Terror Hotbed Pak more Biz-friendly than India," September 13, 2005. http:www.hindustasntimes.comnews, and "Not Businesslike," http:www.businessstandard.comstorypage
16. See http:www.cybernoon.comeditorial, September 16, 2005.
17. Informal post-presentation interaction with Dr. Srinivasan and other experts gave valuable, additional insights into why China is performing considerably better than is India in terms of economic advances — be it in the GDP growth rate, progress of the manufacturing sector, share of global international trade, or attracting foreign direct investment.
18. "India's Promise," *Harvard Magazine,* July-August 2005. http:www.harvardmagazine.comonline070591.html
19. *Common Sense Government Works Better and Costs Less, Op Cit,* p. 22, Introduction.
20. "Civil Service in Transition," Lecture delivered at India International Centre; excerpted in *The Pioneer,* October 26, 1999.
21. "Reading Between the Lines for an Honest Babu," *The Indian Express,* May 14, 2002.
22. "An Unlikely Alliance," *The Hindustan Times,* July 28, 1996.
23. See Anup K. Datta, "Looking Back: Greedy Bureaucrats," *The Statesman,* May 14, 2006. http:www. thestatesman.netpage.news
24. "India Among Most Corrupt Nations," *India Abroad,* (Weekly), New York, October 29, 2004.
25. A preview of the impressive study was provided by Prof. Jenkins at a seminar on *The Politics of Anti-Corruption* held at Johns Hopkins University's School for Advanced International Studies (SAIS), Washington, DC Campus, on February 17, 2006.

26. "Public Services Reform," May 14, 2002.
http:www.india-seminar.com 2002514

27. "Draft Freedom of Information Rules a Joke," says CHRI, September 10, 2004.
Human Rights Initiative, http:www.infochangeindia.org

28. "Right to Information Inaction," *The Indian Express,* March 2, 2006.

29. National Colloquium on Right to Information, held at Bhopal on December 12, 2005.
http:www.news.webindia123.com

30. Alan Sipress, "In Indonesia, Local Campaign Against Graft Ignites National Effort," *The Washington Post,* October 4, 2004, p. A-18.

31. "Six Trends Transforming Government," IBM Corporation, September 18, 2006.
http:www.businessofgovernment.org

32. *Memoirs of a Civil servant, Op Cit,* pp 57-58.

33. Some senior officers, known to be very close to the top leaders and enjoying their patronage, are referred to as belonging to their group — *The Rajiv Gandhi batch* or *The V.P. Singh batch* (both Prime Ministers), and the like, rather than their service batch (the starting year of their service), as per usual practice. Madhav Godbole refers to a cartoon which pithily shows a civil servant addressing his colleague: "I belong to *The V.P. Singh batch,* you must be of *Rajiv's."* See "Civil Servants: Serving the Master," *Op Cit.*

34. Quoted by Arun Shourie, "Filing the State Away," *Op Cit.*

35. "Reading Between the Lines for an Honest Babu," *Op Cit.*

36. India: Asia's Next Tiger?" *Essays in Public Policy,* Hoover Institution, September 10, 2004.
http:www.hoover.stanford.edupublicationsepp82c.html

37. In my university job, I took the initiative to modify the earlier transfer policy to make it just — and not a carrot/stick deal to favour/punish teachers, researchers, extension workers, and other employees. With extension offices in every district of the state, several research centres, and a college for undergraduate studies in another town, the university administration could use transfers to improve efficiency through optimum allocation of human resources, or misuse the system to *teach a lesson* to the teachers and other employees who were not in the administration's good books. This discretion was substantially circumscribed — if not totally eliminated — under our revised, objective transfer policy.

38. "Depoliticise India's Steel Frame," *The Hindustan Times,* August 1, 2004.

39. The chief secretary of U.P. told Dharma Vira that "your father had specially requested me to transfer you and I have done it". To this the latter responded: "If that is the case, then I would like the transfer order to be cancelled...I

don't want that I should be spoon-fed by an influential father. I can look after myself." (*Op Cit,* pp. 14-15)

40. During my latest assignments in India, and even in the post-retirement days, I received a large number of requests from friends and relations for influencing the authorities to make a particular transfer or to cancel one; some of these requests did have merit and some none at all; I remember one case where a lower-level employee unsuccessfully requested me to help with his transfer to a far away place. What he did not tell me was the fact that the scope for illegitimate gratification (bribes and favours) was greater there than in his current posting close to his house!
41. "Fall of Bureaucracy: Greed for Power and Wealth is the Main Cause," *The Indian Express,* April 3, 1993.
42. "Evolution of Metapreferences in the Indian Bureaucracy," *Sanjiv Sablok Term Paper, ECON 538,* December 4, 1995.
43. "A Troubled Venture," *The Indian Express*, September 4, 1995.
44. "Civil Servants: Serving the Master," *Op Cit.*
45. "M.N. Buch on Civil Servants,'" *The Hindustan Times,* October 4, 1995.
46. "Indian Bureaucracy in the Next Millennium," Talk delivered at a Panel Discussion of Delhi Administrative Officers' Academic Forum, held at India International Centre, New Delhi, November 21, 1998. http:www.cuc.nic. inuscvcspeeches98nov4.html

CHAPTER IX

1. I was told the *Meenas* of Rajasthan is one such community. This reminds me of another community that in earlier years appeared to have a proportionately large number of members in the Foreign Service — Kashmiri *Pandits,* especially the *Kauls;* that *merit-based* concentration became the subject of a joke in diplomatic circles: There are three *cols* in the country's Foreign Service — proto*col*, alh'*col*, and Kashmiri *cols (Kauls)!*
2. It is surprising that no systematic, credible study has been done regarding the effectiveness of long-running reservation policies in order to answer important questions such as the following:
   - Are the policy goals being achieved?
   - How are quotas affecting performance; the performance of reserved-category candidates vis-à-vis those from the open category?
   - Characteristics of training; what is its success rate in making reserved category candidates compete well with open category candidates?
   - What are the implications of any performance evaluations for the training curricula and methodologies adopted, and for the content and conduct of civil service competitive examinations?

- What are the effects of the policy, on inter-caste and inter-class harmony — on the overall social fabric of the country?
- Would alternative policies achieve the desired objectives equally well or better?

These are tentative questions; experts on different aspects of administration and evaluation/survey techniques should be able to devise proper, bias-free assessment procedures.

3. No wonder a wag once suggested: Why not declare *all* castes, tribes, etc. in India backward?!
4. As stated by a well-known journalist, M.J. Akbar (Editor-in-Chief, *The Asian Age,* New Delhi), "To seek reservations in the private sector, as some backward militants insist on doing, would become a negative burden on growth…There have to be other means through which we can straighten the imbalance of decades."

   "Shrinking Jobs for Muslims," December 21, 2006.
   http:www.dawn.com20061221ed.htm
5. T.A. Johnson, "Quotas no Answer," *The Indian Express* (U.S. Edition), May 12, 2006.
6. "Quota Question," *The Indian Express* (U.S. Edition), May 26, 2006.
7. "Moily Heads Panel on Quota Implementation," *The Hindu* (Online Edition), May 30, 2006.
   http:www.hindu.com20060530stories
8. Aziz Haniffa, "Pan-IIT Alumni Campaign against Reservations," *India Abroad* (Weekly), New York, November 17, 2006.
9. The Sachar Committee Report on Indian Muslims is available widely on the Internet.

   See, for example, http:www.zmag.orgcontent, December 2006.
10. "Minority Report," *India Abroad* (Weekly), New York, December 29, 2006, p. A-15.
11. See, for instance, commentaries by Badri Raina and Dileep Yogi.
    http:www.news.education4india.com1974, December 31, 2006.
    http:www.desicritics.org20061214, December 14, 2006.
12. "Prejudices and Preconceptions about Muslims in India: Writing on the Wall," *Asia Times,* December 21, 2006.

    http:www.forum.atimes
13. "Shrinking Jobs for Muslims," *Op. Cit.*
14. "Quota Is not the Best Way To Bring People Up," December 28, 2006.

    http:www.news.education4india.com1974the-rajendra-sachar-commission-report-missing-facts

15. Hardwari had actually written that Dr. Rajendra Prasad "must be turning in his grave" — a questionable statement in the light of the Hindu custom of cremation rather than burial.

16. "Favouritism Ruins Civil Services," *The Hindustan Times,* June 9, 1995, Op Ed page.

17. I got to know Hardwari Lal well when he was advising in the late-1980's the Indian Council of Agricultural Research/Central Ministry of Agriculture on affairs of State Agricultural Universities. Although he had his share of detractors, I found Hardwari Lal to be a keen observer — an analyst *par excellence* — of political and social issues.

18. The U.S. practices have obvious applicability because of the past, severe discrimination against minorities resembling the injustices done in India to segments of the population on the basis of caste and other factors.

CHAPTER X

1. Quoted in J.R.D. Tata's biography. See *Leadership Digest,* September 17, 2006.
   http:www.careerage.comleadershipvol1art10.shtml

2. Besides other material, information on reform proposals contained in the following references was found useful:
   - "Radical Proposals to Change the Face of Bureaucracy," *The Hindu,* August 19, 2004.
   - "Better Governance: Some Straws in the Wind," Sumer Kaul, August 20, 2004.
     http:www. samachar.com
   - "Will P.M. Succeed in Ensuring Good Governance?" Surendra Mohan, August 21, 2004.
     http:www.samachar.com
   - "Too Much Procedure Means Corruption," Interview of Cabinet Secretary B.K. Chaturvedi by Naresh Taneja, *The Times of India,* August 29, 2004.
   - "Parallel Reforms Launched to Reform Bureaucracy," IANS, September 16, 2004.
     http:www.newindpress.com

3. On the subject of district/regional planning, for instance, a good deal of work has been done (and published) at the academy. I once presided at a daylong seminar on Area Planning held there and found the quality of work and discussions of high quality — comparable to the work done in that field at some universities and other institutions. Discussions with faculty members during another visit indicated that the Academy is keeping up

with latest developments in its widening field of interests, e.g., environment and ecology, which were engaging my attention at the time.

4. I know of one directorate in the central ministry of agriculture which sent *a very large proportion* of its senior officers (from Economic & Statistical Adviser, Deputy and Assistant Advisers, down to the level of Research Officers) to the FAO in Rome (and other international agencies), turn by turn, during the early- and mid-1960s — the period during which I was working at Delhi. I personally know more than half-a-dozen of them. They usually went for short terms but almost all of them ultimately managed to get absorbed in regular jobs. While some of them were certainly competent (also holding advanced degrees from reputed Indian and foreign universities), some others didn't have meritorious backgrounds, academic or otherwise, and were no match for many of the analysts who had worked with me at the university in the fields of agricultural economics and statistics/ econometrics — policy analysis, welfare economics, agricultural development, economic projections, etc. — that are highly relevant to the work of FAO.
5. "Are IAS, IPS Model Services?" *Op Cit.*
6. I remember looking at the well-prepared theses of two of my departmental secretaries in Pondicherry — Pradip Mehra and Parminder Singh — who had studied in the United Kingdom.
7. *The New Dictionary of Thoughts,* Hanover House, 1956, p. 552.
8. For details of the order see the Court's Judgment (on Civil Writ Petition No. 310 of 1996 — Prakash Singh & others, Petitioners *Versus* the Union of India & others, Respondents) and some good commentaries, e.g., by C. Ratheesh Kumar and by R.K. Raghavan.
   thehindu@web1.hinduonnet.com
9. "Government Constitutes Second Administrative Reforms Commission," Press Release by the Ministry of Personnel, Public Grievances & Pensions, August 31, 2005.
10. Nistula Hebbar, "India Plans new Administrative Reforms Panel," August 23, 2005.
    http:www.rediffmail.com
11. Another cause for worry? The superstitious ones amongst us would have preferred a 12-point or 14-point terms of reference, rather than 13!
12. Fakir Balaji, "Administrative Reforms to Be Technology Drive, Citizen-centric," *Indo-Asian News Service* (IANS), September 8, 2005.
13. "Government Needs Managerial Mindset," *India Abroad* (Weekly), New York, July 18, 2003 (Excerpts from the Govind Ballabh Pant Memorial Lecture delivered in Pune).
14. Once — a joke goes — when a senior bureaucrat was given a very good proposal which, additionally, had the merit of being practicable, his response

to the presenter was: "Glad to know it would work in *practice,* but does it work in *theory?!"*

15. "The India Model," *Foreign Affairs,* July/August 2006, U.S. Council for Foreign Relations, New York.
16. As an example of resistance to innovative thinking, I would like to cite personal experience from my days as Vice Chancellor of CCS-Haryana Agricultural university. I felt that, as part of our agricultural extension activities, we should not only advise individual farmers but also attend to their group needs, including advocacy on their behalf, when justified. Lobbying for fair demands put forward by farmers' associations would thus fall within the purview of our extension/developmental activities, or so I believed. However, a number of my colleagues seemed to have different ideas as was revealed when a group of poultry farmers came to us to formally put their complaints/requests at a meeting of poultry experts — from the university as well as from outside. One of their demands was to secure for them lower than prevailing electricity rates for poultry house operations. This obviously involved lobbying the state government on their behalf, and I assured them we would take their case to the concerned state authorities. However, after the meeting ended, a couple of university participants had reportedly murmured: "V.C. Sahib is adding *unnecessary* work to his very busy schedule!"

CHAPTER XI

1. Many, if not most, taxi drivers love to *go out of their way* to help you!
2. "The India Model," *Op Cit.*
3. According to a light-hearted description by Nicholas M. Butler, "An expert (specialist) is one who knows more and more about less and less." A frivolous take on it: add to the above — "until he knows everything about nothing!" Then a generalist would be one who knows less and less about more and more until he knows nothing about everything!
4. "Can We Improve Public Service Delivery?" September 9, 2005.

   http:www.financialexpress.com
5. CIOL News, April 7, 2006.

   http:www.ciol.comcontentsearch
6. N.C. Gundu Rao, "Pruning the Bureaucracy; Flab and Fatuousness," *The Deccan Herald,* July 29, 2003.
7. "Sixth Pay Commission May Derail Economy," February 9, 2006.

   http:www.RediffIndiaAbroad.com
8. In the London borough of Bexley, the local authority's architects, street sweepers, ground keepers, and refuse collectors had taken this privatization route by 1995, and other units were looking at it as well. See *Banishing*

Bureaucracy: The Five Strategies for Reinventing Government, Addison Wesley Publishing Company, Reading, Massachusetts, 1997, p. 134.

9. In Haryana, for example, the Director of Agriculture used to be an IAS officer (during the late 1980's when the author was working as Vice Chancellor of Haryana Agricultural University). Most likely, the practice is still continuing, denying the state's agricultural officers the well-deserved chance of becoming even the director of the department. Under the circumstances, becoming Secretary to the Agriculture Department is not even a distant dream for the unfortunate souls!

10. Among other qualified outsiders who came to civil services at senior levels, are: Montek Singh Ahluwalia and Nitin Desai who served as secretaries of economic departments and now occupy even higher positions. The former is the Deputy Chairman of India's Planning Commission; Nitin Desai had moved to the United Nations to work in the field of environment.

11. In the case of granting arms licenses, for example, the collectors/deputy collectors have discretionary powers which, more often than not, leads to corruption. I heard the case of a collector who approved a large number of revolver licenses on his last day in a western district of U.P., collecting a tidy sum of money from each applicant. Such corruption can be easily eliminated — at least reduced substantially — by taking away the discretionary power and defining the minimum criteria for approval of an arms license: say, holding position as a Class II government officer, a mid-level business executive, an assistant professor, a professional paying income tax in a specified range (this would reduce the number of applicants substantially as tax avoidance — by now refined into an art-form — is rampant), or a farmer owning so much land, and so on. Moreover, renewal of licenses should be automatic and the period for each renewal increased to, say, ten years; for the purpose of weeding out some dangerous license-holders through frequent renewals, we are subjecting all law-abiding persons to undertake frequent trips to the secretariat, which — besides waste of time and resources — invariably involves greasing the palms of clerks and peons whose behaviour covers the range from beggarly appeal to *dada*-like pressure tactics.

12. *In Spite of the Gods: The Strange Rise of Modern India, Op Cit,* pp. 66-68.

13. *Banishing Bureaucracy: The Five Strategies for Reinventing Government, Op Cit,* pp. 21, 22, 135.

14. *The Christian Science Monitor,* May 23, 2005. http:www.csmonitor.com20050523

15. "Democracy's Drawbacks," A Special Report, *The Economist,* London, December 19, 2006. http:www.economist.com

Appendix

Press Release — October 8, 2004

A Rare Look at Bureaucracies: A Lecture Series with Gravitas and Shared Personal Experiences

Role of Bureaucracies in Economic Development and Foreign Affairs

Scholars, diplomats, community leaders, students of public administration, and other interested participants in the Washington, D.C. area (USA) were given a rare glimpse of knowledge on bureaucracies during an event hosted on October 8, 2004, by Deen Dayal Upadhyaya Foundation, the U.S.-India Forum, and the School of Public Policy at George Mason University, Fairfax, Virginia. It was an afternoon of introspection, analysis, and a look at prospects, which was a treat for all those in attendance. The excellent list of speakers gave insightful lectures on a timely and important topic: "*The role of bureaucracies in economic development and foreign affairs*". The speakers were: Ambassador Har Swarup Singh, ex-Governor of Pondicherry (India); Mark Doboga, Deputy Associate Director, U.S. Office of Personnel Management (OPM); Neeraj Prasad, ex-member of the Indian Administrative Service (IAS), currently serving as a Senior Operations Manager at the World Bank; and Raymond Vickery Jr., former U.S. Assistant Secretary of Commerce. The moderator was none other than Hon'ble Stephen Solarz, ex-Congressman, the first member of the India Caucus in the U.S. Congress, and one of the most pro-India political leaders in the United States.

The afternoon began with remarks by the founder of the US chapter of the Upadhyaya Foundation, Shekhar Tiwari, and by Parag Shukla, Executive Director of the chapter. They reminded about the valuable work and life of Pandit Deen Dayal Upadhyaya — a noted political thinker, scholar, writer, and journalist — and told about the Foundation's Annual Lectures where outstanding experts holding diverse views are invited to discuss a wide variety of topics. During the past quarter century of the Foundation's work, the approach has been one of open enquiry and absence of presumed orthodoxy of views.

In his introductory remarks, ex-Congressman Stephen Solarz highlighted the importance of the seminar topic, focusing on his personal travels and experiences in countries of South Asia — particularly relating to their bureaucratic systems.

The first speaker, Mark Doboga, talked about the role of the U.S. Office of Personnel Management, various reform efforts made over the years, and transformational guidelines for strategic human capital management in the 21st Century. He underscored the importance of preserving the organization's ideal: "The core of the system, codified in statute and regulated by OPM — *the merit principles* — must not be compromised." This aims at ensuring that any future reforms will continue to be grounded in these fundamental principles. Doboga's presentation was followed by a brief commentary by Dr. Kathleen Suneja. She said that "the layers of bureaucracy cause gridlock and jealousies over turf between bureaucrats which prevents them from freely sharing information with their colleagues and delays day-to-day decision-making or frequently no decision-making at all."

Ambassador Har Swarup Singh, who spoke next, felt that India's bureaucracy had contributed a lot towards *stability in administrative functioning* despite worrisome *political instability* during some periods in the country's post-Independence history. However, he maintained that "the record of civil services in achieving social and economic advancement leaves much to be desired, pointing to the necessity and urgency of undertaking bureaucratic reforms." Some specific recommendations made by the speaker included: recognition of the worth of technically qualified people *(technocrats)* by giving them status, powers, and monetary rewards comparable to those accorded to *generalist bureaucrats* (of the IAS and Allied Services), and recruiting reputable experts for senior civil service positions from outside. Dr. Singh pointed out that "the Indian administrative model allows IAS officers not only to monopolize senior-most administrative posts but also to head a large number of public-sector entities and even some institutions of higher learning, for which they usually do not have the right credentials." The speaker stressed that "this *administration/control-centric* approach, in preference to today's much-needed *development-centric orientation,* is holding back the nation's progress."

The third speaker, Neeraj Prasad, talked about the challenges faced by the Indian Administrative Service in the 21st Century. He stated that "a unique combination of selection methods, early training, and placement in challenging field assignments generates a breed of bureaucrat who is expected to be all things to all people, usually with remarkably successful results, but not without some less-than-perfect endings."

Both speakers on Indian bureaucracy proposed reforms to improve accountability, efficiency, and responsiveness in the country's civil services, and to banish corruption. They drew upon their long and distinguished record of administration and personal experiences — both inside and outside the civil service — which was insightful and rewarding to listen to. Dr. Sudhir Wanmali and Joginder Kumar gave comments on these two presentations, highlighting major, intractable bureaucratic problems.

Finally, Raymond Vickery spoke on bureaucratic entanglements that hinder the smooth flow of trade between the countries of South Asia and the United States. He wondered whether "the Indian bureaucracy built for a Fabian economy can implement free market-based economic growth." Mr. Vickery shared his intimate personal knowledge of trade relations and of the day-to-day functioning of the civil service in India that apparently continue to impede better commercial ties between India and the U.S. Narasimha Koppula commented upon Vickery's presentation — expressing hope that the incipient reforms would be expedited. This rounded off an evening of informative and thought-provoking presentations.

In his concluding remarks, Hon'ble Solarz praised the organizers for arranging the seminar and the speakers for their lucid, analytical, and constructive comments on a subject that has a vital bearing on the various issues of democratic governance, and on the conduct of foreign relations. He felt — based on observations during his numerous visits to India — that "broadening and energetically pushing forward administrative and economic reform measures would contribute significantly to India's development."

Amod Desai moved a vote of thanks — for the organizing committee, outside volunteers, and the sponsors of the lecture series. With this ended the function for this year. One will now have to wait a year or so for another set of presentations in the lecture series of this high quality and noticeable value, mainly for the benefit of India.

The function was held at the School of Public Policy of George Mason University's Arlington campus in northern Virginia.

INDEX